...more songs
the radio
won't play...

...more songs the radio won't play...

STAN ROGAL

poems

Published by ECW Press
665 Gerrard Street East
Toronto, Ontario, Canada M4M 1Y2
416-694-3348 / info@ecwpress.com

Editor for the Press: Michael Holmes / a misFit Book
Copy editor: Crissy Boylan
Cover design: Jessica Albert

MISFIT

Earlier versions of some of these pieces have been published in *TRAIN: a poetry journal*, *Talking About Strawberries*, *Subterranean Blue*, *Acta Victoriana*, *First Literary Review-East*, and a 2021 chapbook published by above/ground press.

LIBRARY AND ARCHIVES CANADA CATALOGUING IN PUBLICATION

Title: ...more songs the radio won't play... : poems / Stan Rogal.

Names: Rogal, Stan, 1950- author

Identifiers: Canadiana (print) 20240496736 | Canadiana (ebook) 20240496744

ISBN 978-1-77041-803-5 (softcover)
ISBN 978-1-77852-380-9 (PDF)
ISBN 978-1-77852-379-3 (ePub)

Subjects: LCGFT: Poetry.

Classification: LCC PS8585.O391 M67 2025 | DDC C811/.54—dc23

This book is funded in part by the Government of Canada. *Ce livre est financé en partie par le gouvernement du Canada.* We acknowledge the support of the Canada Council for the Arts. *Nous remercions le Conseil des arts du Canada de son soutien.* We would like to acknowledge the funding support of the Ontario Arts Council (OAC) and the Government of Ontario for their support. We also acknowledge the support of the Government of Ontario through the Ontario Book Publishing Tax Credit, and through Ontario Creates.

This book is dedicated to Selina Martin,
a good friend and terrific musical talent (with a great set of pipes)
who definitely deserves more air time: rock on!

All of literature is a series of references and allusions.
— SUSAN SONTAG

These Songs are not meant to be understood, you understand. /
They are only meant to terrify & comfort.
— JOHN BERRYMAN

Why can't we sing songs like nightingales?
Because we're not nightingales and can never become them.
— JACK SPICER

Contents

Bonus Tracks

Author's Note

In this collection, I've attempted to take formerly popular tunes (from various genres) and transform them by applying certain postmodernist techniques and tropes, most specifically self-reference; mixed discourse ranging from the erudite to the profane; allusions to other arts and sciences; biographical and historical facts (or bent facts or gossip) pertaining to the particular original artist and/or their times — including their own specific influences/borrowings in some cases; snippets of philosophy and literary theory; quotes and quote bastardizations; recycled language (much of it likely considered non- or a-poetical, yet, when placed or reframed in a different context . . . well, who knows?); enjambment; sampling; off-kilter humour; and so on, all in an effort to update and *perhaps* make relevant to a present-day audience. While (unavoidably) serving to comment in some way on popular music/culture/lifestyle/politics, there is no main "theme" or "message," and the true emphasis is on the process and/or style of writing, not the destination but the journey that is of significance, allowing the reader to attach their own thoughts and experiences to the mix and arrive at their own conclusions, if such are desired. Not mere cover versions, not parodies, exactly (though parodic), but redactions, mutations, Frankensteins, if you will, which somewhat (vaguely?) resemble the original, yet are grossly different, and with the hope that the particular artists accept these burnt offerings as tributes. Taken as a group of "singles" composing a longer "compilation," i.e., the "book" or "record," there occur echoes throughout, thus making the whole greater than the sum of its parts — a gestalt, to varying degrees — yadda yadda.

"PARENTAL ADVISORY: Some songs contain certain expletives which may offend some listeners. All words in these songs are part of the songwriter's vernacular. If you prefer not to hear certain words, one idea might be to memorize the recording so you may anticipate any words or phrases you find undesirable and then either press the mute button on your stereo or create a loud noise by yelling or dropping a noisy object onto a hard surface until you are certain the offensive lyric has passed."

— SELINA MARTIN

The Rain, the Park, & Other Things
The Cowsills

knew I had to say hello [hello, hello]
droning a drowsy syncopated tune
speech impregnated with a rhetoric absorbed through the airwaves
to lighten. make light of. to arouse elation, buoyant ascension
[insert here the aleatory decay of sound]
I mean, in terms of describing love or longing or libido
     what does each look like?
          what shape, what colour?
               what coarse wale of warp & weft?
if text is the electricity that moves the body from one thing to another
what are the results of being relentlessly specific?
literally momentary?
all the parts are more like plumbing fixtures
than pieces of a poem
a clear example of "songs & dances of social allusion"
that is: music which however danceable & "swinging"
          remorselessly contrasts social imperfections
               against implied criteria for perfect living
well, why didn't you just say so?
suddenly, the sun broke through [hello, hello]
pussy willows big, their tops above water
green & red leaves flat against the branches
whatever it was she was wearing — *poof!* — gone
was she reality or just a dream to me? [hello, hello]
object dissolves into a field of loose relations
flowers in her hair, flowers everywhere
at the point of ceremonial sex (no touching, no tongue)

     we stand starkly naked at the edge, singing

One Thing Leads to Another
The Fixx

there's no glory in uncovering, the fix is on
as when the wrong word goes in the right ear
&/or . . .
      as with a hand uneasily holding the knob of a door
(wearing green fingernails & gold handcuffs)
false starts & dead ends are inevitable
often, it's more a matter of the particular *cut*
a kind of latticework sieve made from split bamboo
the sparking arc of a smoked-to-the-filter butt
something there is that doesn't love a wall
       the broken eggs, the maimed doll, the blindfolded figure
         the dizzying vortex of beating wings & flying drapery
clear examples of "suspended accentuation patterning"
[off-beat phrasing of melodic & choreographic accents]
perplexed by these excerpted sentences
      — why not [*just*] say what you mean, mean what you say? —
where one thing can be substituted by another thing, it's no go
the merry-go-round, no go the rickshaw
the works on display all have some function
they exist without either frame or pedestal
[the *author* here (please note) is conveniently absent]
pretty soon the stage is a scene of muted carnage
bodies of dolls arrange themselves in frankly erotic reconstructions
the kill floor resembles a red sea that tides in & out with the moon
in the morning light a line
      — it's the year of the cloud, when my marriage failed —
[antidote is a bone in the throat : one thing leads to another]
     a garden covered in thick marble instead of snow
        a shave-headed man nailing shingles to the sides
of a glass house

Friday I'm in Love
The Cure

Another manic Monday, can't trust that day
Nothin' really wrong, just feel I don't belong
Emergent theme of unsettling otherness
Twilights of androgyny & inattention
Wanna shoo-*ooh-ooh-ooh*-oot the whole day down
Sun comes up, it's Tuesday morning
Tuesday's a heartache, love comes, love goes
Lying with you, you turn your face from me
Tuesday afternoon I'm just beginning to see
That's right, you're wrong; you're wrong, that's right
Anyway, I'd rather listen to Coltrane
Than go through all that shit again
Waiting for Wednesday, Wednesday morning 3 a.m.
Watch my chest gently rise, gently fall
Now straight, now slightly bent
As yesterday was the day for watching
A universe tethered to the corporeal form
A fulcrum between scales of the heavenly body
& temptations of the flesh
We used to meet every Thursday, remember?
In the afternoon, for a coupla beers, a game of pool, &
— well . . . one thing leads to another, yeah? —
But that was then
I won't wear makeup on Thursdays anymore
I'm tired of covering up
But, hey, it's Friday, I'm in love
Saturday begins the same as other days
But ends up different in many ways
It's the Saturday night special
Got a barrel that's blue & cold between my teeth
10:15 & the tap drips under the strip light
Drip, drip, drip, & I'm sitting at the kitchen sink alone
A discursive visceral wondering

Should I kill myself or go bowling?
Oh, Sunday morning
You sure have changed since yesterday
Sunday bloody Sunday, let's go
The real battle's just begun
Another day like every other one
But, hey, it's Friday, I'm in love
Shift away from sombre elegy toward satiric exuberance
Complete with flapping louvres & retinal scans
A universe of clichés so familiar
That they seem at once comforting & strange
An inscrutability of purpose & yearning that jostles
The underside of meaning
Such an easy beat
Within an atmosphere of pop glamour
& celebrity fetishism
Tonight, I'll spend my bread
Tonight, I'll lose my head
They call it stormy Monday [but Tuesday's just as bad]
Wednesdays there's no cure, Thursdays can't endure
Saturday, Sunday, draw the blinds
But, hey, it's Friday, I'm in love

You Turn Me On, I'm a Radio
Joni Mitchell

. . . what kinda music you turned on to? . . . movement, slippage, &
collision . . . as in a film by Godard: yr alone in a car, speeding along a
deserted section of flat sun-scorched asphalt with its mirage of rising
wavy lines, at the wheel of an Alfa Romeo, top down, wearing an
expression of cynical neo-capitalism & cruelty; wearing white socks &
a pale blue windbreaker, one of those "beautiful boys" drinking Coca-
Cola & smoking a Gauloises; a nasty mix of revolutionary socialism
with the still warm ashes of a dying Catholic faith, you become a
free-floating signifier of the mythology of American masculinity . . .
a "quantitative expression" of a "measurable transference of [e]motion"
. . . tickled to the short hairs . . . what serves to multiply the erotic
potential of the central mood . . . you send yr message loud & clear
. . . dream maker/heartbreaker . . . "you turn me on, I'm a radio, I'm
a broadcast tower waving for you," &ETC, et cetera, same old same
ol' familiar euphemistic party line tune . . . you spin the dial madly
through the garbled frequencies . . . a wind of milk & blood whistles
static over the borderline airwaves that marries melodrama to post-
punk goth rock, dead wave & doom metal, J-pop & hip-hop, corny
country & smooth jazz, bubblegum & classic, garage & grunge, reggae
& new wave synth-pop, court & spark . . . amid the snap/crackle/pop
buzz, "the Text" becomes a multi-dimensional space in which a variety
of writings — none of them original — blend & crash, a collection
of [generally] atavistic eructations, crepuscular & fragmentary [in
fact, the lone lonely singer often appears dissolute & disassembled
passed out on a bar stool enhanced only by the implacable yellow &
white grid that serves as a backdrop] . . . the wisteria's in flower, star
of Bethlehem, wild geranium & hepatica, clamour of woodland roses,
hissing of summer lawns . . . it's the season of love, baby . . . why is it
then that I feel so goddamned fucked up? . . . there are darker things
beneath the lilies, the antelopes & the blue monkeys . . . eggshells of
spells, incantations, bewitchments, & further voodoos . . . rumours
that each pretty young lady of the canyon stashes rusty hairpins &
razor blades up her quim to ward off undesirables . . . not that that sort

of thing ever bothered you or ever got in yr way, no . . . it's been dirty for dirty down the line . . . then again, what'll tell yr future when you blast all the stars from out of the sky, huh? . . . but, hey, honey, one hand washes the other, yes? though I don't expect the ghosts of radio past will ever again transmit suggestive messages into my restless daughter brain . . . too bad, so sad . . . some get the gravy, some get the gristle, *yeah*, *yeah*, *yeah* . . . on the night ride home many people on the bus sleep the whole way, others sit staring holes into the air, others plan rebellion, music flooding designer earbuds, volume pumped . . . what bravado impelled me to come here without the comfort of my own plastic pocket-sized transistor, I wonder? . . . ah well, no regrets coyote, something got achieved once upon a long time ago — ecstasy — why go further?

A Whiter Shade of Pale
Procol Harum

Cue the necromantic erotic anatomy lesson
Wave & particle, particle & wave
Under pressure of situational torque
It enacts an economy of perambulation & coincidence
Replete with Bach-like breaks & atmosphere
An actuator in the heat coil, really
Thick outlines, bright colours
Pizzicato & sempre pianissimo e senza sordino
Tuned in perfect fifths

[Chorus]
A lusty tale of the errant G-string*
Amid a protocol of pale & mirthless harems
Such a cool cat beyond these things
Hot on the counter-tenor cello plucking rhythms

From this observation we turn to consider passion
Here we are busy exercising our prerogatives
A skilful evocation of tension between diverse objects
Ultra-rapid forms of free-floating control
Linguistic conventions with sparks of irony
Where a quick shuffle of bourré does the trick
Slipped the jack of diamonds dusk insinuates itself
A sound more melancholic than amorous
Set loose against the pitch

[Chorus]
A lusty tale of the errant G-string
Amid a protocol of pale & mirthless harems
Such a cool cat beyond these things
Hot on the counter-tenor cello plucking rhythms

---

*   Johann Sebastian Bach's "Air on the G String"

I'm the Boy
Serge Gainsbourg

I'm the boy that can enjoy invisibility
A bit of mottled blue behind a skin of fog after days of grey
Hello. Hello! It's me. Who else?
The one who seems ever trapped in the beauty of a bourbon cloud

I'm the boy, a see-through toy
A [semi] solid structure of repetitions & permutations
Afflicted with an almost castrati-like voice
Frantic to build vast Babels of scalar variants

Face flushed a little, head muzzy
Smoked again, drank again, counted the cigarettes, the glasses
This is the beginning of obsession
Where a shift in the concept of sexual identity is essential

Let us pause to consider . . .
"The Somnambulist" or "Secrets of a Necromancer"
Phonemic density coupled with semantic openness
An ability to shine & wing when in doubt

A visionary impulse at once sensual & deprived
Dreams are now a pathway to the banal
Sexual abuse that is part of the larger political oppression
That unfolds like so many stock film shots

Sure, I looked [What am I saying?]
Behind the curtain, under the bed, looked & looked again
In the ominous the numinous awaits, yes?
Seeking evidence of the illusive orgasm

Sounding complaints of logorrhea
A hail of vitriolic trash talk & angry bullets
New doors that soon turn into old walls
The commonplace Byronic heroes & Gothic villains

Between roses & shadows on a foreign earth
The work becomes a celebration in darkness
I climb down into my feet to become
An anonymous footprint in the sand

I'm the boy that can enjoy invisibility
A bit of mottled blue behind a skin of fog after days of grey
Hello. Hello! It's me. Who else?
The one who seems ever trapped in the beauty of a bourbon cloud

A Day in the Life of a Fool
[a.k.a. Manhã de Carnaval, a.k.a. Samba de Orfeu]
Carl Sigman

A day in the life of a fool
Below wooded eyebrows the thunder means business
The paper that was once a tree cries for its leaves

> *. . . they asked me how I knew a shade of blue was blue . . .*

Things take their immutable course with calculated movements
What requires a slippage into that fugitive closure

Nothing behind the door, behind the curtain
Where bodies are the furniture of dreams
[A portion of the text is missing here, likely to do with loss &/or
sadness; likely containing an internal rhyme (see initial stanza):
    "something . . . something . . . something . . ."]

> *. . . & yet you don't believe her when she says her love*
> *is dead you think she needs you . . .*

Too many unreal movies, too many passions clutter our lives
Between the genitals & the brain there are only exploding bridges

[Long instrumental break featuring Luiz Bonfá on guitar,
    George Albert Shearing
on piano, Carl Sigman on flute, Marpessa Dawn on maracas
    (& backup vocals)]

"Each in his bed spoke to himself alone, making no sound"
On my back smoking, a radio turned up loud in the next apartment
. . . verlassen, verlassen, verlassen, bin ich . . .
Every day in the life of a fool

Vissi d'arte

Maria Callas

"As you will recall from our last thrilling episode of Puccini's opera, Tosca, *the painter/lover of Tosca, Cavaradossi, has been captured, tortured, & threatened with execution within the hour by Scarpia, the chief of police. Tosca pleads with Scarpia, even offers him money, to release Cavaradossi. He flatly refuses, then offers his own proposal: the life of her lover in return for sexual favours. Having no choice, Tosca agrees. He turns to his second-in-command, Spoletta, & tells him to arrange a mock execution that will be 'as we did with Count Palmieri.' Spoletta nods & exits. Tosca then insists that Scarpia provide safe conduct out of Rome for herself & Cavaradossi immediately following the charade. He easily agrees to this & walks to his desk to draft a document. 'Just tell Cavaradossi to make his death look good,' he says. As he completes the letter, Tosca picks up a knife from the supper table. When the man approaches her for an embrace, she stabs him to death. 'This is Tosca's kiss!' she says. When the stage for the execution is set, the rifles fire, & Cavaradossi drops theatrically to the ground. 'What an actor!' says Tosca, admiring his performance from a distance. Once the soldiers have left, she rushes to the body, only to find her lover dead — Scarpia has betrayed her. [Theatrical pause] & so, let's now listen in to the famous aria that accompanies the action."*

Today's such a bitter day
It wears the cellular lines of release stripped raw
Are you a wind instrument, are you breath?
Who pursued music [& love] with an enthusiasm
that bordered on the pathological
No, I'm not a clown & if my face is pale
it's from shame
Forsaken, forsaken, forsaken, am I

But, hey: insomma . . . it is what it is
Things fail to signify in isolation
& no good deed goes unpunished
Let's go, let's debate marginalization within the social milieu
Let's discourse autotheory* as ontological hermeneutic**
A bowl of flowers [tulips, yellow] seems to be listening
O, I was brilliant, sweet Jesus I was brilliant
Known to face the world unfeathered & alive
What am I now except an unwelcome emission
A vulgar odorous eruption that violates standard practices
A "one who [once] could charm the pants off an angel"
Make it real, they say: real? *Real* as compared to what?
No, I'm not a clown & if my face is pale
it's from shame
Forsaken, forsaken, forsaken, am I
But, hey: insomma . . . it is what it is
Things fail to signify in isolation
& no good deed goes unpunished

---

*   Autotheory is work that engages in thinking about the self, the body, and the
    particularities and peculiarities of one's lived experiences, as processed through
    or juxtaposed against theory — or as the basis for theoretical thinking. It strips
    the pretension of neutrality, of objectivity, away from the theorizing voice.

** Hermeneutics is the theory and methodology of interpretation, especially
    the interpretation of biblical texts, wisdom literature, and philosophical texts.
    Hermeneutics is more than interpretative principles or methods used when
    immediate comprehension fails and includes the art of understanding and
    communication.

Diamonds & Rust
Joan Baez

at this juncture [g'wan] admit the unwashed phenomenon
the troubadour legend, the original vagabond, glory, glory
one of those beautiful equations, almost visible, almost green
half a black rock displaying brilliant crystals

as juxtaposed against the materialistic pig of a technological world
reborn as [yet] another tongue sloshed in too many mouths
drawn to running oblique, funny, vulgar, non-poetic language
(if honeyed, this suckles; if hammered, this spins)

a stinking shit pile of pure potentiality awaiting articulation
possibilities of music set against the rising tide of conformity
a maze of species abuzz in the green humming of trees
of black leather on the dream's black leather jacket

to uncover the sweaty hulk like just the other day
serious mouth, unbrushed hair hiding black eyes
the rose petals arranged over the naughty bits *just so*
the disembodied head ever sensitive to diverse ways of seeing

shoulders, hair, & tongue distributing misinformation
nonetheless worshipped, full of Karma, ambitions, & cash
it's on television & in the streets even when the walk is casual
"look more" it sez; call att'n if menace is the number of so many teeth

there is glitter beneath the wires, the wind, & it is all ok
[g'wan] fry an egg on that famously hot ass, then pick up the phone
the voice is an act of illimitable self-construction
its outline scarred in snow which the sun will later heal

The Dangling Conversation
Simon and Garfunkel

. . . in the newspapers, on the radio, in daily conversation at the office, in the home, over coffee with friends, in the bedroom . . . [so on & so forth example after tedious example, yadda yadda, *snap!*] . . . the impetuosity of language often leads one astray . . . presented in such a manner as to be both suggestive & questioning . . . "the sand is not quite white: granite sand; grey*ish*" . . . others size you up, faces pinched, hands interlaced or in their pockets . . . mad mixture of knee-jerk disbelief from the social neverland performing a kind of linguistic violence on the text & on the listener . . . what bulks large is a strong element of the phatic . . . "can analysis be worthwhile?" "is the theatre really dead?" . . . try putting words in another's mouth even knowing "the other" does not exist . . . go ahead, try . . . every attempt to determine or convey meaning entails some organization of experience in terms of likeness & difference . . . Hume's notion of the primacy of the impression in creating ideas . . . for the purposes of this particular conversation why don't we name that vagueness [the first images need not be excessively dramatic]: two strange white flowers — shrivelled now — & brown & flat & brittle . . . the condor ablaze black-lighting the Andes . . . soap bubbles that move & shimmer & move . . . an automatic pistol tucked in its holster of burnished Italian leather . . . [nota bene: many of the references are drawn from Sufi mysticism, the object being to forever remain free of accountability] . . . "neither reason nor rhyme scheme within this form," some someone said with stunning offhandedness . . . tall with deep brooding eyes & soft-spoken & introverted in unfamiliar settings . . . [um, hello, it's me, uh, how are you, nice weather we're having, I, um] . . . lost . . . lost in the dangling conversation . . . the blurred [bleary] borders of our lives . . . the superficial sighs . . .

Sunday Mornin' Comin' Down
Kris Kristofferson / Johnny Cash

Another funky Sunday
A cigarette & a window-framed silhouette helps set the mood
Serious mouth, unbrushed hair hiding dark brooding eyes
Early in the a.m. Got a beer buzz on. All lit up
  & no place to go. Might also be in the cold & sweatless
meathooks of a
(wouldn't doubt)
psychosis
   the wizard quickly jinxed the gnomes before they vaporized
   uh-huh, uh-huh
From the bottle to the bottom
A path of steep drops & forgotten luggage
   [Insert here ambient sounds: sleepy city sidewalks,
    slow-moving traffic, floating conversations, distant sirens,
    lonely church bells, barking dogs . . .]
Dear _____: somewhere someone's having
   a birthday celebration someone's getting married
    someone's getting laid
Somewhere janitors are watching
grainy movies of men & women urinating in stalls
With the atavism of barefoot people — hola! —
     everyone (everyone) is promiscuous upstairs
The animal leaves its scent every moon every moan
God is absent from (such) considerations of meaning
   [I imagined I saw a mouth jeering, a smile
    of molten red iron running over it, its laugh
    full of bent & rusty nails, rattling]
Here exists the machine set to replicate itself
A vast suspension of undifferentiated inscription
All that is funky, the bubbles bubbly in the monster's conk
What is not funky is psychological, metaphysical
Is the religion of squares
Not worth the powder it takes to blow it all to hell

I mean, how negotiate the shift from quiddity to ideation, huh?
Spring with its promise of winter & the black ivy once again
The doctor's cold metal ear pressed against my chest, listening
Ba-boom, ba-boom, ba-boom . . .
Clouds part & the sun turns into a coffee mug or a doughnut
Paper peaches are tears, mistakes are revelations
Music plays over the radio
[Would a song do better to repair the brain or?]
Getting up from the desk to secure a turkey sandwich
& silence the phone, Man in Black wailing:
  "gonna make it right
    gonna make it right, when I'm in heaven"
I have my finger on the pulse of something
The bridge, the sea, the song of the train
Black leaf mouth of the redbud chewing
Ba-boom, ba-boom, ba-boom . . .

Sweet Emotion
Aerosmith

Sweet emotion . . . Sweet emotion . . .

You talk about people you've never seen
A "one bereft of class consciousness or sense of history"
It's so serious today, the party's over, or haven't you heard?
We're bleeding out, & while you deliberate, bodies accumulate

Do you encounter your own existence?
Do you feel de trop? Is there nausea?
Blest with a carefully calculated apocalyptic aesthetic
Mystery offers its little paw & wags its tail

Sweet emotion . . . Sweet emotion . . .

Many faces are desperate, others smoothed over
A constitution of tissue & marrow & formaldehyde
The pregnant pause & the billowing skirt on the line in the wind
Hey, baby, if you don't like the way I drive get off the sidewalk

Marked by insidious facial scarring, by vicious dog bites on the ass
Wanna wanna make hot monkey love with you
Laid out flat & naked on the bathroom tiles
I met you to slaughter me again & again
& slaughter turns to luxury & luxury turns to ecstasy

Sweet emotion . . . Sweet emotion . . .

Teenage Wasteland
The Who

> "'This music crept by me upon the waters.'"
> — T. S. ELIOT

Arrested by an abrupt minatory staccato
of ponderous monosyllables
A dizzying vortex of beating wings & flying drapery
Enigmatic images that serve to penetrate the lizard brain
What bulks large is a strong element of the phatic
Hey, you — don't walk on the turnips!
Good God, when will they ever learn it?
The broken fingernails of grubby hands
Don't cry, don't blink an eye
It's only teenage wasteland

I set off, I take up the march, I set off
I put my queer shoulder to the wheel
I rush out as I am & roam the streets
Unreal town under the brown fog of an autumn dusk
Dance of death across a chalk-grey sky
Then comes a memory, a rope, a string of jittery lights
Town's end that peters out to rats' alley
Where the dead have lost their bones
Down Greenwich Reach, past the Isle of Dogs
Let's go, let's go, & make our visit
Don't cry, don't blink an eye
It's only teenage wasteland

In the mountains, there you feel free
Where there is no water, only rock
Gonna go south in winter, gonna tan beneath a new sun
Gonna spit out all the butt ends of my youth
I'm no Prince Harry meant to take the fall
I'm the Fool, that's all

These are the pearls that were his eyes, look!
Oh, there will be time, there will be time
What's that noise? Who are those hooded hordes?
Those who arrive to cultivate the fog
Spend a penny on the ailing old guy why don't you
Jug-jug to dirty ears
Don't cry, don't blink an eye
It's only teenage wasteland

Private Idaho
The B-52's

Hoo hoo hoo hoo hoo hoo hoo hoo . . .
Slept away much of the afternoon
The perfect example of a couch potato
Narcoleptic, secure, unaware, then woke with a bang
Out of control, a river that roils & rolls
To be this much in love is to be sick, & I love to be sick
I stare in the mirror: dark circles under the eyes
The dull vacant look of a crushed cigarette butt
Full of tragic gestures — so painfully comical
Caught up in that old "Shakespearean Tragedy Rag"
Walking through the gate that leads you down
Hey, avoid the road less travelled, keep off the grass
Forget the continuum hypothesis & the axiom of choice
You aren't paid, the work is hard, why even bother?
Then again, why shouldn't a quixotic Kazakh jog barefoot along the road?
Each of us is made of welded chrome, buffed & shined
Still expect from music an added degree of depth in that exploration
    of coldness
        which is *dark* love: a yellow concrete landscape, a yellow fish by Klee
           a yellow bird by Akeboshi
Overhead ominous hawks glide like a squadron of B-52 bombers
Each with a plump rat clutched in its talons
Imagine a hard steely nail as a symbol of nakedness, exciting yet dangerous
A musing on the word rubber & the erotics of erasure
Something bald & mustachioed with the crafty movements of a cat burglar
A hand disappearing between legs
I mean, I never knew I was being groomed to be the sex toy of a narcissist
Where even the tenderest kisses have the aftertaste of ash
[Though it is very pretty to love a pretty person, no?]
To be this much in love is to be sick, & I love to be sick
Too bad, so sad, out of control, a river that roils & rolls
Hoo hoo hoo hoo hoo hoo hoo hoo . . .
Walking through that gate that leads you down

The bottom of a bottomless blue blue blue pool
Underground like a wild potato
My own private Idaho
Nun freut euch: all rejoice, all rejoice
My own private Idaho
Hoo hoo hoo hoo hoo hoo hoo hoo . . .

Mexican Radio
Wall of Voodoo

[I dial it in & tune the station . . . faint sound of a radio announcer speaking in Spanish in the background . . . I can't understand, what does he say?]

. . . the white bellies of fish are a weird excitement . . . the kitten shows itself bloodied from some small mouse . . . a river nudges Coors Light beer cans into the reeds . . . crows talk back in their black velvet voices . . . limestone & pine : a dry country : lightning-eyed . . . splattered like an egg of fire . . . hovered uneasy on the edge of allegory . . . they have strange licence plates & engines that devour America . . . technological presence of bodily comfort & abominable fear . . . the white peacock roosting might have been Christ . . . this country (a nation on no map) . . . it exists as image — a rugged Marlboro Man / riding a palomino quarter horse / across an unspoiled landscape / whose day is done . . . the new age now exhausting the fertility of the semen . . . p.s.: aside the obvious inflammatory, remarks : I still plan to travel, still plan to holiday in / olé! / Mexico . . .

. . . faceless thieves chuckle & stumble & embrace beer cans & butts, choked beneath a mushroom cloud in the year of the roach . . . children, dogs — the street is thick with their running — who plunge themselves under the meat truck looking for an egg . . . skin is sufficient to be skin, that's all : an abyss, then, an imbroglio / drooling at the mouth hole / *clickety-clack* of wooden teeth . . . the cancerous ghosts of old con men shed their leaves . . . the yellow moths sag against the locked screen doors . . . gradually houses splinter to the ground in red & white . . . come on now touch me babe in this waking dream . . . boots sound the floorboards : your tears are real water, burning . . .

. . . sun baked provocative women, slender, like whips of sex . . . the girl you left in Juárez, dress-torn by the misadventure . . . old women, knitting, breathless, tell their tales . . . they send up black smoke between the shadow & the sun . . . ugly dreams of natural functions : flippered arms & perfunctory fingers unroll the map of love to make Psyche

weary & Eros weep . . . gunslinger urinates like other men : suffers /
brute necessity / under the tulip roots figured a way to be a religious
animal / a long-horned bull : half-man, half-deity : half-drunk, half-
mad . . . jacked off to a staticky Tex-Mex pop-tart tune . . . keep it real,
compadre . . . all around is evidence he is not in hell — yet — behind
the wheel of a '47 Cadillac / took out his own forehead . . .

You're So Vain
Carly Simon

You enter a room, how?
Aloof, sure, you don't give a shit, why should you?
All eyes are on you while yours are in the mirror.
Please don't confront me with my failures.
I had some dreams, so what?
The whole thing has the smell of the trashy filmed novel about it.
Sunny mornings with a café con leche & a jelly doughnut.
That's how it goes, pure inspiration, no method,
a little cocaine.
It's not about you, no, it's not about you
[but it is]

You know, don't you, that you talk incessantly?
I mean, is it the ease of technology, or what?
A kiss is something I might get behind.
Restless nights in one-night cheap hotels.
A porno-*cum*-horror-snuff flick on the tube.
Another emotion-free brand of distortion & distraction.
That's how it goes, pure inspiration, no method,
a little cocaine.
It's not about you, no, it's not about you
[but it is]

I see you made the cover of *Rolling Stone*.
Funny, you're no rock star, so who'd you fuck?
Never mind, I'm not naive.
You tip your hat, use your scarf like a garrote.
Losing track is fun the first time, but . . .
Listen up, fool, you're not head of Parks & Rec anymore.
Making it on the beach with the lonely tourist trade.
Collecting orgasms in jars to use as night lights.
Still. Why should I care?
There's always another bus around the corner, right?

That's how it goes, pure inspiration, no method,
a little cocaine.
It's not about you, no, it's not about you
[but it is]

Blue Angel [sonnet]
Roy Orbison

"Oh, blue angel, don't you cry"

in the manner of solipsism & prayer
the tense imperfect future of it is the condition
that things *will have been* other than they were
a mythology of recognition & revelation
somebody loves somebody & that somebody doesn't
or somebody loves less or loves somebody else more
fraught with lurid relations & failed suicide attempts
in this mastered light, creature absorbs creator
are you a wind instrument, are you breath?
send in the clowns, the flash mobs
moth-like in mist, scintillant in the moment's wrest
how a cunning stunt slips the tongue between sobs

sha la la, dooby wah, dum–dum–dum, yeh yeh, um
sha la la, dooby wah, dum–dum–dum, yeh yeh, um

Sex (I'm A . . .)
Berlin

jesus! what gorgeous monkeys we all are
smoking below the stone of flesh
we recognize & are recognized by:
        "the circumambient swarm of parasites
        or *thermal exciters* we emit, simply"
feel the fire, feel my love inside you, it's so right
say *what* now?
[love is no comfort(er), rather, a nail in the skull]
childhood being a fascinating euphemism
       for iron maidens, pillories, & executions
          the whole notion of eating, eating, eating everything
I put it to you — who hasn't used a cellphone to attain sexual satisfaction?
there's the sound & smell of it, slip it in
got a mouth like a sailor
I'm knackered, I'm bitchin'
I'm an all-day sucker, I'm a snack
I'm a toy, come play with me
I'm a virgin, I'm a whore
I'm your worst nightmare, I'm your mother
I'm what gives your hands something to do when the lights go out
what of this evil? what operetta?
conceptualism wants you to know it has read Lacan
flarf is a smutty, expressive, swan-bear hybrid at a clam bake
I mean, you don't have to be a drug addict
       pederast, sadomasochist, or nitwit to enjoy
          the performance (but being one or more would likely help)
okay, right back into it, the endless musics, a necessity
          — a ballad of emotional/sexual dependency —
reel it in & shut your cake hole

I'm knackered, I'm bitchin'
I'm an all-day sucker, I'm a snack
I'm a toy, come play with me
    I'm a toy, come play with me
        I'm a toy, come play with me . . .

Comes Love
Billie Holiday

Why, baby, why, baby, why, baby, why?
Questions of the soon-to-be slain.
Where fat grim orange jack-o'-lanterns leer
& empty vases you endow with flowers
fill the gloom.
That's all, brother (don't try hiding).
Comes love, nothing can be done.

It's a cheating situation, yes?
Love shall be blonder, slimmer, younger.
Will be the bomb, the door in the wall,
an offer of instantaneous intimacy,
of perpetual (e)motion.
That's all, brother (don't try hiding).
Comes love, nothing can be done.

Ah, sweet easing away of all edge, evil, & surprise!
The sometimes mouth that masticates or gags.
Everything that acts is actual.
(I believe it's the auratic quality that sucks one in).
Comes a sad song, give your nose a little blow.
Comes the devil, you can tell him where to go.
Comes love?
That's all, brother (don't try hiding).
Comes love, nothing can be done.

Sweet Dreams (Are Made of This)
Eurythmics

Strange stranger the sweet stuff of dreams
The cloud-capped towers, the gorgeous palaces
Is it or isn't it pleasing not to be enjoying
By the little piece of string, by the ocean travel

Having & reiterating is where it is at
Primitive signals still speak to us
Buried creatures of sly erasures
The dark & light place where flowers grow

Syntax erupts & flows lubriciously around
Its conventionally obstruent limitations
Sweet dreams that are the guardians of sleep
Androgynous w/ close-cropped orange-coloured hair

. . . feeling & coming, feeling & going; you're an angel & you gave me
your love; feeling & coming, feeling & going; anyone kissing is one
needing kissing; feeling & coming, feeling & going; you're an angel
& you gave me your love; feeling & coming, feeling & going; anyone
kissing is one needing kissing; feeling & coming, feeling & going;
you're an angel & you gave me your love; feeling & coming, feeling
& going . . .

Strange stranger the sweet stuff of dreams
The cloud-capped towers, the gorgeous palaces
Is it or isn't it pleasing not to be enjoying
By the little piece of string, by the ocean travel

Having & reiterating is where it is at
Primitive signals still speak to us
Buried creatures of sly erasures
The dark & light place where flowers grow

Syntax erupts & flows lubriciously around
Its conventionally obstruent limitations
Sweet dreams that are the guardians of sleep
Androgynous w/ close-cropped orange-coloured hair

. . . feeling & coming, feeling & going; you're an angel & you gave me your love; feeling & coming, feeling & going; anyone kissing is one needing kissing; feeling & coming, feeling & going; you're an angel & you gave me your love; feeling & coming, feeling & going; anyone kissing is one needing kissing; feeling & coming, feeling & going; you're an angel & you gave me your love; feeling & coming, feeling & going . . .

I Just Came to Tell You That I'm Going
Serge Gainsbourg

I just came to tell you that I'm going
Love must be continually reinvented it's plain
In a vacuum all bodies fall at the same rate of speed
A wind of milk & blood whistles the rooftops
So it's bye-bye blackbird, so long, farewell

Looking for someone to save you
I can't save you I can't save myself
Something hit our heads & our heads hummed
Connected by apophenia, only, a feeling
Of abnormal meaningfulness
A cause replete with carcinoma & ragas
Okay, fine, I come as I go, I came as I went

[instrumental break with background humming provided by singer]

I just came to tell you that I'm going
Love must be continually reinvented it's plain
In a vacuum all bodies fall at the same rate of speed
A wind of milk & blood whistles the rooftops
So it's bye-bye blackbird, so long, farewell

Looking for someone to save you
I can't save you I can't save myself
Something hit our heads & our heads hummed
Connected by apophenia, only, a feeling
Of abnormal meaningfulness
A cause replete with carcinoma & ragas
Okay, fine, I come as I go, I came as I went

Looking for someone to save you
I can't save you I can't save myself
Something hit our heads & our heads hummed
Connected by apophenia, only, a feeling
Of abnormal meaningfulness
A cause replete with carcinoma & ragas
Okay, fine, I come as I go, I came as I went

[*instrumental break with background humming provided by singer*]

I just came to tell you that I'm going
Love must be continually reinvented it's plain
In a vacuum all bodies fall at the same rate of speed
A wind of milk & blood whistles the rooftops
So it's bye-bye blackbird, so long, farewell

Looking for someone to save you
I can't save you, I can't save myself
Something hit our heads & our heads hummed
Connected by apophenia, only, a feeling
Of abnormal meaningfulness
A cause replete with carcinoma & ragas
Okay, fine, I come as I go, I came as I went

[*repeat verses if so inclined, ad hoc, ad nauseam, ad infinitum*]

[& yr bird can sing] [a compilation]
John Lennon

Entertainment critic & journalist Robert Fontenot states that the lyrics of "And Your Bird Can Sing" are among "the most speculated-upon of any Beatles' track." Music critic Jonathan Gould says that Lennon wrote the song about Frank Sinatra. He refers to an article by writer/ journalist Gay Talese who described Sinatra as "the fully emancipated male" & repeatedly mentioned his use of the word "bird" in the piece to mean "penis." [you say you've heard every sound there is & your bird can swing.] Sinatra himself said he was "tired of kid singers wearing mops of hair thick enough to hide a crate of melons" meanwhile having an assistant dedicated to maintaining his own 60 "remarkably convincing" hairpieces. Singer Marianne Faithfull said the song was addressed to Mick Jagger & written about her, since she was Jagger's girlfriend (or "bird" in English slang) at the time. [when your bird is broken, will it bring you down.] According to *Rolling Stone* magazine, & supported by writer Kenneth Womack, the line "you say you've seen seven wonders" could be a reference to a comment Paul McCartney made in 1964 when the Beatles were smoking cannabis with Bob Dylan in New York. Photographer Robert Whitaker based his photo *Birdcage* on the song's lyrics. The cage was among the props assembled by Whitaker for the 25 March 1966 shoot featuring the Beatles in butchers' smocks & covered in dismembered dolls & raw meat. [Paul later turned vegan: okay fellas, quite brisk, moderato, foxtrot!] Lennon's first wife, Cynthia, recalled that the song was inspired by her presenting him with a clockwork bird inside a gilded cage. She wound up the bird as she presented it to him so that it sang, leaving him with "an expression of sheer disbelief on his face." According to Womack, Lennon viewed the caged imitation bird as a metaphor for his marriage & a reflection of Cynthia's inability to understand him. They separated soon thereafter. [when your prized possessions start to bring you down.] Writer Nicholas Schaffner commented "perhaps John was still under the influence of Bob Dylan, who at the time, seemed to take pleasure in confounding dissectors of his 'message' with cryptic lyrics that made no sense at all." *Mojo* placed the song at number 41 on its list of greatest 101 Beatles' songs. English academic Toby Litt admired its Indian drone quality & the raga influence in the guitar melody. He identified the track as "the birth of all power pop, from Big Star through Cheap Trick to Fountains of Wayne & the inspiration for other artists that use jangle to attack." Steve Marinucci of *Billboard* described the song as "incredibly ambitious, highlighted by a superb guitar solo." Thomas Ward of *AllMusic* describes the song as one of the finest on *Revolver*. Rob Sheffield of *Rolling Stone* writes that despite Lennon's dislike of it, "And Your Bird Can Sing" is "one of the finest songs ever" describing it as "scathing . . . yet also empathetic & friendly." Musician Phil Collins highlighted the song as "one of the best songs ever written & only a minute & a half long." [you say you've seen seven wonders & your bird is green.] John Lennon called it "another of my throwaways . . . fancy paper around an empty box." [but you don't get me, you don't get me, okay, okay, okay (okay, okay, okay).]

Radio Ga Ga[*]

Queen

> "William Blake is eating stars
> & one, very slowly,
> Brightens inside my mouth"
>
> — CLAUDIA KEELAN

If honey, this suckles; if blood, this delights
Waters turn from ice, creek is aroar
Another of those beautiful lost nights
Pure strambotto beneath the covers
Almost visible, almost green
Twilights of sexuality & inattention
An inscrutability of purpose & yearning
Toward the pink underside of meaning

Noted for its sonic & lyric intensity
Radio spins demented through the spectrum
A pandemonium of paradoxical symmetries
An atmosphere of pop glamour & celebrity fetishism
Where confusion is general or at least mutual
Teenage nights roused by devil music & spirituals
Never immune to the lure of flesh & glitz & awe
— Lock, clamp, release, dissolve, then snow —

---

[*]   Written in the Tuscan folk verse form rispetto (a version of strambotto).
    Rispetto means respect in Italian.

Sunday Will Never Be the Same
Spanky and Our Gang

what kinda music you on now, anyway?
ruby-throated, spanky clean
      dressed in bright scarves & flowing chiffon
            fern-like eyes, cheeks the rosiness of flowers
where "sun" & "rain" are the commanding metaphors
that have no use for either burning giraffes or fur-lined tea sets
images suspended against cracked & dripping surfaces
works that are monumentally visible, legible, & accessible
that have as much aura as its references
the classic boy-meets-girl / boy-loses-girl (or vice versa) scene
[we'd walk together hand in hand]
by the public hook for the private ear become a total
"stroll in the park"
banality as key to exploiting the masses
the bridge coolly lifted from "Les anges dans nos campagnes"
accompanied by flute, harpsichord, & cello, natch
— Gloria in excelsis Deo —
(s'okay, s'alright, I don't believe in God
      so I don't have an issue, steal away)
            . . . *baa-da-da-da-da-da-da-da* . . .
so on & so forth

what is the object of all these songs
fuzzy 'round the edges & kinder
      (shall I compare them, then, to a summer's day?)
no need to uncover the function of a complex variable
dreadful has already occurred
as when the canary in the mineshaft squawks, no one listens
Zen'ei geijutsu ni tsukaremashita [I grew tired of avant-garde art]

a gang of angels roams the countryside in fright wigs packing axes
— in hindsight one risks becoming what one critiques —
I mean, even dogs are (often) Shakespearean in their doggy ways, yes?
[the "sun" is gone: the "sun" is gone & I think it's gonna "rain"]
— Gloria in excelsis Deo —

      . . . baa-da-da-da-da-da-da-da . . .

[I wanna be sedated]
Ramones

What a difference a day makes
Twenty-twenty-twenty-twenty-four little hours
Who used to be the shit now ain't worth shit
Hard on the outside numb on the inside that's me
Nowhere to run to baby nowhere to hide
Today you're young, too soon you're old
Christ, this bitter earth can be so cold
Oh quick quick quick
Don't make a big fuss
Toss me in a wheelbarrow stick me on a bus
I wanna be sedated

[chorus]
Where there was sunshine & flowers now there's just rain
Where there was love & romance now there's just pain
I'm goin' off the rails I'm goin' insane
Put me in a sleeper car on that crazy train
Hey hey nah-na-na-nah nah-na-na-nah
Hey hey nah-na-na-nah nah-na-na-nah
I wanna be sedated

There are darker things
Beneath the lilies & the antelopes & the blue monkeys
Things that take their immutable course with calculated movements
Where each new thought appears either absurd
        or threatening or anachronistic or deceptive
Today you're young, too soon you're old
Christ, this bitter earth can be so cold
Oh quick quick quick
Along the highway of fallen horrors sits a ghost
Flag me down a taxicab ship me parcel post
I wanna be sedated

[chorus]

A cut rose, a dead polytechnician, what could be sadder?
Alarmed by its sordid violence & rudderless drift
Every existing thing is born without reason, prolongs itself out of weakness
    & dies by chance
When the stars enter the horizon that's Tuesday gone — hey presto, like
    that!
Today you're young, too soon you're old
Christ, this bitter earth can be so cold
Oh quick quick quick
Even the Romans remain a part when the generations slip
Strap me to a stretcher get me on a drip
I wanna be sedated

[chorus]
[repeats]

White Rabbit

Jefferson Airplane

almost Alice
short skirt / long jacket
white rabbit tattoo on her inner thigh
do you *wanna wanna* touch me?
eat me? drink me?
[I like you so much better when you're naked]
      — she got that poodle tongue, that thumbnail pant —
what begins with performance
a certain slick grace
a documentary aesthetic that conveys street style
note: all photographs are memento mori
scissored at the neck
a bizarre case, certainly [though]
      imprisoned by her parents in a room of walled mirrors
      attacked with paddles, a hacksaw, a pocket watch
      a select assortment of savage skeletal creatures
the girl who tumbled down the hole, drank the wine, dropped the pill
complicated by overtones of incest & child abuse
a mythologized vision of the salvationary heroine
cheek laid soft against the surrealistic pillow
burned for the last time
[honest, I only smoke when I'm in bed with you]
sure, doll, sure
when logic & proportion have fallen sloppy dead

              white knight's talking backwards
              red queen's off with her head

who is/was [essentially] one extended crescendo
almost Alice
    almost Alice
        (when she was just small)

Turning Japanese
The Vapors

so I saw what I saw
cut & shapeliness
padded shoulders & knife-edged trousers
the erect nipple centred in wax
mouth studded with tiny white teeth
   — *Our Lady of the Cherry Blossoms* —
the delicious thrust & relaxation
following the curves of cast-iron balconies,
   sniffing dogs, the movement of women's blousy skirts
so nature's radiation appears
an angel layered in cake
stretched out on a bed of sushi cooler ice
lovely & cold
where history of the eye seems this side of taboo
    — so, what of this evil? what operetta? —
whether the oriental riff or Aladdin's quick step
neither the impulse to kitschy uplift nor the love of eeriness
in isolation the effect is crueller, a victim of vagabondage
"I am borne darkly, fearfully, afar"
a desire for murder of the normal
who must imbibe semen but in imagination
what happens when we are robbed of the right to good feelings
(a clear case of the vapors)
bewilderment as a poetics & a politics
hear the shaped scream of days in the hole
   turning Japanese, turning Japanese, yes,
   I really think so
accessories finger each other
we no longer know if we mimic or are mimicked
[sound & lights (sudden) go out in the cell block]
terror dissolves into image, thus,
   my voice is empty
   "blurred" & "breathless"

Hallelujah

Leonard Cohen

. . . topic varies but tone & extension are epic . . . part heartache part arousal part don't give a flying fuck . . . absolute torch & twang . . . the protagonist is male w/ female characteristics &/or vice versa . . . his/her sin is a cinema of seeming . . . a one well acquainted with the tools of falsehood & propaganda . . . grappling the interstitial mark between abrasion & adumbration . . . semantic drift & mid-morphemic rapture . . . beneath & betwixt the narcissus roots figures a way to be an wholly religious animal . . . here is the machine set to replicate itself from used materials . . . something w/ green pastures & keening birds . . . answer its breathing by dialectical probation . . . *hallelujah, hallelujah* . . . almost constant concern to reconcile polarities into manifestations of flow, circuits & cycles, relations & concordance . . . combining elements of goth rock, darkwave & doom metal . . . fanaticism of detail that leads from reconstruction to destruction of the self . . . the exactitude of the slur, the flaw, the stumble . . . [too soon the "I" writing & the "you" reading are become missing persons in the shifting langscape] . . . not a lesson but a lessening; a loosening . . . — *it is perhaps well to write down warnings frequently,* sd saint kafka; *there is hope but not for us* — . . . uh-huh . . . oscillatory sink & segregatory float . . . toothcombing tenacity . . . less alcohol, more fasting, less sleep, more methamphetamines . . . imaging fish leaping through walls of burning water . . . [are you a wind instrument, are you breath, well, are you?] . . . for some time now secretly writing songs kept in an old wooden cigar box . . . the work a celebration in darkness, at once weird & refined, scatological & lofty, comic & serious, ETC etc. . . . — oh, allow me [please] to fry an egg on that [*most* serious, here] most perfect hot ass — . . . *hallelujah, hallelujah* . . . disclosure seductively defers itself, slippage is a primary modus operandi [never a fan of the poetic muse, per se, baffled by buttons & zippers, was soon brought to knee] . . . complaints of severe logorrhea lying spread-eagle, naked, face up, forming sexless snow angels on the frozen ground, no action down below, no holy dove moving . . . "I will never condescend to be a mere object of turbulent & decisive verbs" . . . &/or: "I'm having trouble with my body, it keeps changing shape, the nipples an eccentric extravagance, the nose a monumental squander, I will get old, demur w/ fur, get cellulite, get pubes, get morose"... so on & so forth, fine ... a clear example of laziness, self-indulgence, selling out ... verlassen, verlassen, verlassen bin icht ... i.e., portrait of the forsaken troubadour as mud-caked corpse ... nothing in my hand, nothing up my sleeve, nothing on my tongue but *hallelujah, hallelujah* ...

Pretty in Pink
The Psychedelic Furs

the morning wets its lips
seemingly sexless but occasionally violent
after the cigarettes, the beer, the wake-up calls
it's late, the bell has sounded
big dumb dogs bark & bark at their boredom of barking
Jacqueline laughs & the sky fills with rain
makes you think her life's a drag
dreams no longer open a pink expanse
they've become grey
breakage, crumble, multiplication of an enigma
when heated the mouth breaks off like an egg
Jacqueline at the disco doing a brand-new dance
dolled up in pink psychedelic fur, pink jumpsuit, pink heels,
chunky pink plastic sunglasses
        night unbuttons virgins & the hour's lost
cute in a dumb-ass sort of way
[& wasn't she easy & isn't she]
pretty, pretty in pink
cultivator of sidelong glances, erections, & soaked panties
trapped in narrow hard spaces of steeled corridors
teenagers get friendly, smoke pot, groove to the music
bloated kids seemingly filled with air & surrounded
by sharp pointed apparatus & gigantic toys
if it all doesn't sound [too much] like a cheap romance novel
or made-for-TV movie:
      the young brides pregnant at the altar
          the grooms drunk & disorderly
              the maids of honour recently laid
parents attend the service packing prayers & shotguns

Jacqueline laughs & the sky fills with rain
makes you think her life's a drag
cute in a dumb-ass sort of way
[& isn't she easy & isn't she just]
pretty, pretty in pink

Radio Nowhere

Bruce Springsteen

Creeping along the highway of fallen horrors
Image of cannibals & headhunters outlined in fog
Airwaves grow thick with sentimental inanities
Screwed & under some voodoo curse
Crepuscular & fragmentary
Land of a thousand dances gone suddenly mute
Where chimneys blow human ashes into the air
It's radio nowhere

Hey, nonny-nonny, hey, nonny-nonny

Gimme border blaster radio stations
Gimme Radio Luxembourg speaking tongues
Gimme the Rivets of Love using power tools as musical instruments
Gimme Don Ho covering "Shock the Monkey" with his mixed
patois of Hawaiian, Chinese, Portuguese, Dutch, & German

A bark sets out at the crossroads
Picking its way across the field of bones
Black milk, burnt bridges, a grave pall to the air
The machines [now] quietly mind themselves
Qui est ce grand corbeau noir?
Free-floating signifier of the American myth
Oh, no, it's not dark yet, but it's getting there
It's radio nowhere

Hey, nonny-nonny, hey, nonny-nonny

Gimme border blaster radio stations
Gimme Radio Luxembourg speaking tongues
Gimme the Rivets of Love using power tools as musical instruments
Gimme Don Ho covering "Shock the Monkey" with his mixed
patois of Hawaiian, Chinese, Portuguese, Dutch, & German

Cruising across a jagged line of misty peaks
The transmitters drone on & on
Who'll speak for these dead who've put their mouths on backwards?
[Insert here an imperfect snapshot of wrongdoing & corruption]
I'm post-bebop. I come from Bud & Bird & Monk
A body filled with carcinomas & ragas
Cannibals & headhunters on the square
It's radio nowhere

Hey, nonny-nonny, hey, nonny-nonny

Gimme border blaster radio stations
Gimme Radio Luxembourg speaking tongues
Gimme the Rivets of Love using power tools as musical instruments
Gimme Don Ho covering "Shock the Monkey" with his mixed
patois of Hawaiian, Chinese, Portuguese, Dutch, & German

Cannibals & headhunters on the square
It's radio nowhere

Slow Motion

Ultravox

You asked [don't ask]
I operate within a fracture; all my surfaces shine, like,
often, see, I'll string a line from my head & see what it sez
Several sentences appear, each sentence enters the situation
created by all the other previous sentences
A flickering begins, as a mouse scampering across a wood floor flickers
Uncanny potency of junctions, spooked transitions of empowerment
Suspended & minor ninth chords for enhancement
Erotic pleasure — *if* it exists at all — is purely incidental
Slow motion
Slow motion

A textual system underlies every textual event
Form follows function; a shift away from the dominance
of anthropocentric scientism
A device that parses & dictates fate
A very hip configuration of angled elbows & light horn-rims
To lighten, make light of, to arouse elation
It is the tango, there is snow everywhere
Slow motion
Slow motion

Today's such a cold blue day
Night is already falling & the damp fog creeps in from the sea
How do you explain this lurking?
After all, we do have sex & other appetites
Grey skies through venetian blinds
The killer asleep in the cabin as the victim photographs him
Slow motion
Slow motion

Walking in L.A.
Missing Persons

What helps pass the time
Hand steady on the wheel, eye on the Strip
Don't be duped by Hollywood theatrics
Machine-gun chatter, radio blasting "Vamos a Bailar"
Buzz-buzz, gimme the yeyo, yeah!
Unlike me, & I do so, so infrequently
A case of missing persons
Haunted, half-dead characters who reduce themselves
to objects

Walkin' in L.A. Nobody walks in L.A.

A soiled undershirted guy walks by
A reedy & subdued Pacino look-alike
He drags a headless corpse behind him, so what?
No one gives a good goddamn, he's a nobody
'Cause he's *walkin' walkin' walkin' in L.A.*
Nobody walks in L.A.

Seniors hit the malls in golf carts
Half-assed actor wannabes cruise the bars on blades
Kids on skateboards, ad execs on Vespas
Cops don't walk the beat, they prowl the streets in squad cars
Everyone tarted up like zombies on a tear

Walkin' in L.A. Nobody walks in L.A.

Maybe it's the heat & maybe it's the ocean fog playing tricks
Maybe it's the angel dust
More likely just another porno-*cum*-horror-slasher-gangster flick
in the classic De Palma style
Whatever, don't be duped by Hollywood theatrics
El hombre guapo el sol amarillo

Unlike me, & I do so, so infrequently
A case of missing persons
Haunted, half-dead characters who reduce themselves
to objects

Walkin' in L.A. Nobody walks in L.A.

Itchycoo Park
Small Faces

slantwise from a station of the Metro
not many in the park today, except
        guilty lovers, stray dogs, & mother nature's child
unleashed
the smell of patchouli & sandalwood
of cinnamon & dust
the smell of the sun & the smell of the rain
a kiss-proof world of motorized wheelchairs
plastic toilet seats, tampons & taxis
ham-like bodies strangled in their Sunday suits
have you searched inside your mouth lately?
the tongue unlocks & won't ease up
[but why the tears there?]
get high, touch the sky
prepare a small face to meet the crowd of faces that you meet
consider a girl who keeps slipping off into the hypnotist's trance
a guy who reads cowboy novels & walks with a limp
the most smiling, most perfumed dreamstuff
of the boldest transcendental artificiality
        (apparition of mad hatters & smoking caterpillars aside)
herds of rhinoceros roam the broad boulevards
pink poodles play on a sofa that stands on a cliff
pale yellow petals cling to wet black boughs
men at the chessboard polish their glass eyes
tune in, turn on, tell you where to go
everywhere the notion of innovative reuse
it's all too beautiful
(stick a needle through my kneecap I won't flinch)
feel inclined to blow my mind
get hung up, feed the ducks

Itchycoo Park it's where I'll be
get high, touch the sky
it's all too beautiful
(repeats . . .)

I'm in Love with a German Film Star

The Passions
  (for Ingeborg Bachmann)

Hello. Hello. It's me, who else?
Bohemian by the sea.
I saw you in a bar, neither elegant nor shabby.
Outside the sexless anonymity of the street.
You were sitting in a corner in imperfect clothes
trying to look indifferent, even bored.
Without ever calling attention by interfering.
Smoked again, drank again, counted the cigarettes.
A real troublemaker.
I'm in love with a German film star.
Oh, my, how unlike a Wittgenstein.
It really moved me, it really moved me.
Yah, it's a dangerous world.

[Fog machine, flashing lights. Instrumental break w/ Echoplex guitar]

Hello. Hello. It's me, who else?
Bohemian by the sea.
Here is the beginning of obsession.
Where sexual love points to the Passion,
the crown of thorns.
Do you want to get together?
Yes, no; now, later; well, what; &, but
Jaz in ti. In ti jaz.
Me & you. You & me.
What do you say?
The limits of my language are the limits of my world.
Für-niemand-und-nichts-Stehn.
Unerkannt, für dich allein.
To stand for no one & nothing.
Unrecognized, for you alone.
Smoked again, drank again, counted the cigarettes.

A real troublemaker.
I'm in love with a German film star.
Oh, my, how unlike a Wittgenstein.
It really moved me, it really moved me.
Yah, it's a dangerous world.

Radio Ethiopia / Abyssinia
Patti Smith

> "Hell is other people."
> — JEAN-PAUL SARTRE

Oh, I got news for you, it's the day of atonement
A kind of hybridization of an urban semantic instrumentality
Rebels slaughtered in a square by machine gun & mortar shells
Who dreamt a carefree boho life in Abyssinia
A world dominated by pastiche & schizophrenia
Cannibals & headhunters, jackals & hyenas
Where frogs get devoured in quantity by almost everything
A crazy-ass bugger with one glass eye, hip shot & lame
Ahhh, something hit our heads & our heads hummed
Buffed & polished, metal plates inserted where we'd been hit
[Jesus, I hate to laugh but I cannot believe]
Able to pick up a radio voice preaching the Gospel "according to"
The thrust is positively geomantic

[Insert here a live performance of the Butthole Surfers singing "We Are the World" complete with video montage containing graphic mob-style execution scenes, nuclear explosions, meat processing, spiders & scorpions stalking prey, gory driver's education highway accident clips, penis reconstruction surgery, bloody roadkill, intercut with panoramas of pastoral landscapes & gently grazing wildlife, elephants & rhinos, flocks of flamingoes, underwater footage of luminous aquatic creatures, as well as a colour negative presentation of a popular *Charlie's Angels* TV episode]

Addis Ababa, city of animal electricity
Much of the work expresses an androgynous auto-erotic
& polymorphous sexuality
Less labyrinthine or rhizomatic than striated

Perhaps I'm a mix of Yemeni or Omani configuration
A third-generation South African of Lithuanian-Jewish descent
Dog-faced baboon screaming from the cage:
"I can't hear you 'cause your mouth is fulla shit!
Waaaa! Waaaa!"

. . . what was I thinking? to oppose with awkward heart all forms of racism, sexism, & cultural chauvinism, to resist all forms of repression & censorship & to defend thereby the acts of the individual (that most local & most threatened form of human life) against the restrictive pressure of the state of organized religion, & of the vigilante actions of those who live in fear among us . . . a genuine concern for contemporary appropriation — an obsessive preoccupation with violence notwithstanding — who had emerged as a dominant poet of the victimized, of the totally discarded & outlawed, imbedded in the city's red light district, its sexual underbelly . . .

Got my feet on bombed ground
Got my sculpted hands 'round the neck of a Duo-Sonic
[I swear on your eyes no pretty words will sway me]
Pressured speech, racing thoughts, flights of ideas
The work supports a fetishized perception
          — Brâncuși's bird, say, ablaze, black-lighting the Simiens —
The awakening blue & yellow of singing phosphores
Strutting the streets of Harar sporting a Rolex
They cracked my jaw, took away my legs, funny
Every act of becoming conscious, she sd, is an unnatural act
Still, I might be tempted to love [or something] if only
But, hey, one monkey don't stop no show, no
Exit slowly, softly like the verdant khat tree
Like the white lily floating down the black river
Like the red benches of a Charleville streetcar headed south
Through the steely grey fog

Real Live Bleeding Fingers and Broken Guitar Strings
Lucinda Williams

Get loose, lighten up
You holler before you're hurt
Not *how* the world is but that it is
Is the mystery
Floating through a palladium
Of mineral ash & anthracite
Waiting in vain for love's sirocco
Where do I stand & how does it feel?
It's real live bleeding fingers
& broken guitar strings
Are you listening to me yet?
Smoking du Maurier Lights & slapping five
Sounding like overloaded bulb wattage
Post-Creedmoor electroshock clarities
Deliberate flattening of tonal register
Extensive use of non sequitur
Coming out in riddles of oracular demon pulleys
& the pregnant pause
It's real live bleeding fingers
& broken guitar strings
Get loose, lighten up
Laughter is the sneeze of the soul
Who'd acquired attributes of promiscuity
& emerged as a dominant poet of the victimized
A one resembling Ingeborg Bachmann
Perhaps it was the poetry
Perhaps the cigarette burns on the arm
[Have you sent for me? Have you sent me this?]
Better, real live bleeding fingers
& broken guitar strings
Real live bleeding fingers
& broken guitar strings

Bang a Gong (Get It On)
T. Rex

what ground is this?
youth's long march; its discontents,
its maladies
studded with lightning bolts
& proclamations

often labelled a young Cassandra-like
acolyte of Jewish mysticism
a very hip configuration
of angled elbows
& light horn-rims

Bang a gong (get it on)

visitor of liquid apartments
at once strange & familiar
no fixed address, fearless
the taxidermied animal
that goes for the throat

notice so many threads
wisely joined together
shot-counter-shot over the shoulder
feel it, a flick of the whip
a brown hand on the red radishes

Bang a gong (get it on)

who are you except
a renegade leggy figure astride a hog
crepuscular & fragmentary
an uncanny potency of junctions &
spooked transitions of empowerment

a more or less conscious plagiarist
[twenty love poems & a song of despair]
graced with the scab-picking concentration
of a child
hey, dirty sweet, yeah, you're my girl

Bang a gong (get it on)

Hungry Like the Wolf
Duran Duran

Here exists the condition of besidedness
A grammatical state of adjacency
Do do do do do do do dodo dododo dodo
The use of portable equipment, hand-held cameras
Non-pro actors, extensive editing, long takes
Narrative ambiguity
Lush & cinematic shots of jungles, rivers,
Elephants, cafes, & marketplaces
Backgrounded by an electronic production
Of guitar-heavy groove, Roland Jupiter-8 keyboard
Roland TR-808 drum machine with sequencer
Blended with a series of instant hooks
A venture that puts an oblique, sometimes apocalyptic
Spin on pop romance in the verses
But keeps the choruses clear & catchy
Where women all have birds beneath their skirts
Hey there, little red riding hood
I'm on the hunt, I'm after you
& I'm hungry, hungry like the wolf*
Do do do do do do do dodo dododo dodo
What kills by fascination, by perverse
Exercise of vision, by the plea of plausible deniability
There are darker things alongside the sacred lotus
The red slender loris & the masked booby
[I always find what I want, see, but when I find it
I don't want it no more, how explain that, huh?]
Are you a wind instrument, are you breath?
Well answer me, are you wild, are you running?
Are you an animal? Look! It howls, flees, hides, waits
A body fit to be prowled over & among
A one endowed with perfect cheekbones &
A generous streak of narcissism
(Roses must grow between her lips, her legs, what?)**

63

Posing is always a little preposterous
But no less enjoyable for that
Time to lace up the boots
& drive the dogs back to the shadows
Hey there, little red riding hood
I'm on the hunt, I'm after you
& I'm hungry, hungry like the wolf
Do do do do do do do dodo dododo dodo

---

*   According to lead singer Simon Le Bon, the lyrics were inspired by the Grimms'
fairy tale "Little Red Riding Hood" & the repeating "do" at the end of each verse
takes its melody from the instrumentals in Gordon Lightfoot's song "If You
Could Read My Mind." Andy Taylor worked out a Marc Bolan-*ish* guitar part,
a very Marshall-sounding Les Paul guitar lick that was added to the track. The
laugh at the beginning of the song & the screams during the song's fade-out
were performed live by keyboardist Nick Rhodes's girlfriend at the time. Bassist
John Taylor stated he didn't really know what the lyrics meant, speculating
that the song is probably about "meeting girls" &/or "wanting to have sex with
someone." Guitarist Andy Taylor (no relation), who contracted a stomach virus
serious enough to require hospitalization from accidentally drinking water in the
lagoon during the music video shoot, described the storyline as a sort of "Indiana
Jones wants to get laid."

     The video was filmed in Sri Lanka (the band had a vision of jungles & exotic
women & Sri Lanka was suggested by music video director Russell Mulcahy, as
he had recently visited the country. EMI spent $200,000 to send the group to the
locale). The jungles of Sri Lanka — oh, interesting sidebar, I think, is that when
I googled the question "Are there wolves in Sri Lanka," Wikipedia's answer was:
Yala, Wilpattu & Udawalawe are just a few national parks where wolves are not
found. Hmmm . . . — evoked the atmosphere of the film *Raiders of the Lost Ark*,
with tip-of-the-hat references to *Apocalypse Now*, e.g., at one point in the video,
singer Le Bon's head rises in slow motion out of the river as rain pours down. The
night before the shoot, Le Bon went to a stylist to get blond highlights in his
hair, but the stylist botched the job & his hair turned orange. That's why he wears
a hat in much of the video. It might also explain why he suddenly gets angry &
overturns a table in a bar. Or not.

     "Hungry Like the Wolf" won the Grammy Award for Best Video, Short
Form at the 26th Grammy Awards in February 1984, making it the first video
to ever win that award. In 2021, *Rolling Stone* listed the song at number 398 on
"The 500 Greatest Songs of All Time."

**   "Roses must grow between their lips." — Virginia Woolf

Broken English
Marianne Faithfull

here is the event horizon
a thing composed of many
nervous movements
& agitated increments
attuned to vulgarity
& violence
in all its sundry guises
go ahead, rattle my cage
shake up my shit
it's a pattern
when it's moving only
trapped in a mirror
of excessive drift
a biker chick, maybe
naked under squeaky leather
astride a speeding Harley, fine
still anything still can still happen
listen amazed
to the radio by the river
state of grace jonesed
that reaches across a distortion
of transmitter waves
voices of indeterminate sex
& cultural backgrounds
an interambient kind of speech
which never fully settles
electric with its patois of
neologisms, archaisms
& etymological dislocations
who are you?
what are you?
why are you here?
what do you want?

did you send for me?
did you send me this?
anyone who is right wouldn't
arrive covered in fog [yet]
disclosure seductively defers itself
slippage is a primary modus operandi
prophecy is an eruption
of the sacred into interpretable form
a long song flows out of the future, noise
from no location[s]
yellow sparks edge the edges
look!
— a plum blossom —
      cold, lonely, puritan
      bluey pink on a live branch
      for which frozen winter
      politely demurs

Private Life
Grace Jones

Dommage si triste with your bullshit
The unexpected comeback almost too perfect
    that sets up the exhausted pissed protest against
        a cult of showmanship & gratuitous virtuosity
Square-cut angular padded shoulders, androgynous
Neo-cartoonish with massive distorting close-ups
Five-foot-eight of wide-eyed raging hard-on
Faithful to the art of forgetting
One of those beautiful equations almost visible almost green
Are you the bomb are you bombed did you bomb?
Great pretender, diva, drama queen
Who suffers strobe light seizures
        & has an abnormal fear of mayonnaise
Your private life trauma, baby, creep me out
Your private life trauma, baby, creep me out
Attracted by your wealth your fame your girlish smile, okay
That time we made hot brutish love in your marriage bed
As accidental as it was inevitable
Well whatever never mind fun's over
Spare me the excuses, the empty diatribe
I'm special, remember? Attuned to the profundity
    of the inchoate world; the one who
        cracks the seashell to release the ocean, *ah*
Telling tales out of school, always the same
An assemblage of ongoing effacements
You speak of "her" (or someone like "her") exhaling corpses
A no-name woman's lip prints on a glass:
        lock, clamp, release, dissolve, then snow
Dommage si triste with your bullshit
Great pretender, diva, drama queen
It's a low-key banger that tips to the fact
Your private life trauma, baby, creep me out
Your private life trauma, baby, creep me out

Poetry Man

Phoebe Snow

(for S___ R____: autodidactic intellectual redneck, semi-reformed)

Don't make me laugh
Born of a fart, fuckstruck
What [who] are you then [except]
    a furious narcissus
           stood naked [unfolded] before a mirror
A more-or-less conscious plagiarist
One foot in modernism, the other in the avant-garde
A creature of formal inventiveness & mannerisms, of weaknesses
& taut gestures
Who resembles some freakishly big, eyeless
        otherwise normal baby who never poops or cries
Scratching phrases across the page in a rapid judder
All your writing is an outburst of peevishness at a world
That refuses to accept you as its Messiah
A clear strong voice one must listen to carefully
To realize what it says is incomprehensible
But hey, it's okay, 'cause you're the poetry man, man
You're a wild thing
You make everything groovy, yeah, yeah, yeah
Lying prostrate on the bathroom tiles
      face down, complaining of severe logorrhea
          deranged by a strange mix of absinthe, opium, hashish
It howls flees hides waits watches
[Talk to me some more, you don't have to go, no]
Leaned heavy on the "complex engagement approach"
Are the pieces you write only enthusiasms?
Tongue fresh from a previous ecstasy so pleasurably flesh
Utterly schmaltzed up with the malady melody
Bend my ear a little, sweets, c'mon c'mon —
      introduce a satisfyingly postmodern element of kitsch
         & sumptuous verse, full of flourishes, & generally empty
Not that it bothers me much [too much]

The sufferings are enormous but one must be strong, yes?
So, speak, stutterer, & stain the page with fragments
You're the poetry man, man [after all]
You're a wild thing
You make everything groovy, yeah

Mama He's Crazy
The Judds

Mama, it's like you always said
Analysis has no access to this condition, love
Sometimes rain, sometimes cloud
Sometimes clear blue sky & that sickle moon
Enamoured of the discursive & the miscellaneous

> *Though too often burned makes me wary*
> *Alarmed by its sordid violence & rudderless drift*
> *Those things that kill by fascination*
> *By perverse exercise of vision*
> *By dialectical probation*
> *&ETC*
> *False starts & dead ends are inevitable*
> *A problem (I guess) when head over heels*
> *Becomes heels over head in a heartbeat*

Ah well, sat squarely on a bullet can't account
For either taste or common sense sometimes
Call me a fool, this one's for real
It's the hour of the expanding man
[Mama, he's crazy, crazy over me]
Serious mouth, lips with a slight sardonic tilt
Unbrushed hair hiding dark brooding eyes
Quarts of whiskey in his system
Blest with a robust capacity for mobile adjustment
Adaptation, & an affirmative renunciation of the enigmatic
I already bought the dream
I'm ready to cross that fine line
[Mama, he's crazy, crazy over me]

Video Killed the Radio Star
The Buggles

> "Music came to a full stop with Brahms; & even in
> Brahms I can begin to hear the noise of machinery."
> — LUDWIG WITTGENSTEIN

Listening intent through the static & hiss
Mouth & ear are in centrifuge & unquiet
Where do I stand? How do I feel?
A mute boy vacuuming up stray music
Just spinning around a dead dial
Whoa-oh, whoa-oh
I hear the DJ, what does he say?
Is there anybody still alive in there?
Gone is Dámaso Pérez Prado's pre-punk hairdo
His "Cherry Pink & Apple Blossom White"
Whoa-oh, whoa-oh
[Video killed the radio star]
[Video killed the radio star]
"Mambo No. 5" gets a MuchMusic makeover
Use of electronics so the voice resembles singing wires
Operatic conventions used to heighten the melodrama
Jump cuts, tracking shots, neo-noir lighting
A dizzying display of smoke, mirrors, & windblown drapery
Who seek a "sublimity of dislocation" toward a
        "new & supposedly enlightened cultural diversity"
Ay pero que rico y sabroso bailan el mambo las mexicanas
Oh, how rich & tasty, the Mexican women who dance the mambo
Whoa-oh, whoa-oh
[Video killed the radio star]
[Video killed the radio star]
Still, for all the techno-glitz & glamour
        it's the genitals the curious tune in to see

A frenzied state of porno passion & ontological anguish
Portable cells in the "wall of voodoo" libidinal nightmare
Deepfake shot of leatherboys Adolf Hitler & Joseph Stalin
      singing high-pitched backup vocals dressed in glittery drag
Qui est ce grand corbeau noir? Who is this big black raven?
Breakage, crumble, multiplication of an enigma
Where no condition is permanent
All the animals peel themselves & turn into synthesized drum pads
I take apart the radio & discover nothing inside except
      glass tubes, foil capacitors, strands of coloured wire . . .
Where do I stand? How do I feel?
A mute boy vacuuming up stray music
Just spinning around a dead dial
Whoa-oh, whoa-oh
[Video killed the radio star]
[Video killed the radio star]

Shock the Monkey
Peter Gabriel

you're agitated, your face is scratched
something flies close by
below wounded eyebrows the thunder means business
cover me, darling, please

small monkeys appear against the flat background
"foliage" finger-painted with monkey guano
[I myself resemble a small monkey]
don't you know you're going to shock the monkey?
hey, hey

I speak [to you] with the singing meat of my brain
I'm nobody's zombie, no snakeskin voodoo doll
oh shit-shaped pain of love bursting in cunt or cock
can't scream 'cause my mouth is full of feathers
can't take it anymore
darling, don't you monkey with the monkey
hey, hey

why not invoke the full harmonic tropical berserk?
psychodramatic catharsis, Machiavellian manipulation
the warmth of a mind not yet neuroleptic but starry & granular
monkey, monkey, monkey
don't you know you're going to shock the monkey?
woot, woot
shock the monkey
woot, woot
hey, hey, yeah

Everybody Knows This Is Nowhere
Neil Young

Going through the mechanics of denotation
Unable to tell if I'm subject or object anymore
A heady mix of revolutionary socialism
      with the still warm ashes of a dying Catholic faith

There are those who'd prefer a modest, more private language
To regard with innocence the outline of a girl in pink chalk on a grey wall
Everybody knows everybody knows everybody
[This is nowhere]

La la la la la la la la la la la la la la la la la la la la la la la la la la la la la
    la la la la la la la la
La la la la la la la la la la la la la la la la la la la la la la la la la la la la la
    la la la la la la la la
La la la la la la la la la la la la la la la la la la la la la la la la la la la la la
    la la la la la la la la

Long ago the story had many birds that passed branch to branch
The cold sea meeting lush agriculture in a romantic embrace
A choice [simply] whether to kill or be killed
      in either the present singular or the past plural

Are you gone wild, are you running, are you gone?
Must silence the ego to allow the world to enter
Everybody knows everybody knows everybody
[This is nowhere]

La la la la la la la la la la la la la la la la la la la la la la la la la la la la la
    la la la la la la la la
La la la la la la la la la la la la la la la la la la la la la la la la la la la la la
    la la la la la la la la
La la la la la la la la la la la la la la la la la la la la la la la la la la la la la
    la la la la la la la la

I'm still the bullet in my daddy's gun
Not broke but badly bent
A psycho-lyrical-photophobic terrorist
        groping for trout in the peculiar stream

Are you gone wild, are you running, are you gone?
Maybe go back home, maybe paint my ass blue or set my head on fire
Oh, no, everybody knows everybody knows everybody
[This is nowhere]

Ooh, ooh, la la la, la la la la, ooh, la la la, la la la la . . .
Ooh, ooh, la la la, la la la la, ooh, la la la, la la la la . . .

The Bottle Let Me Down
Merle Haggard

Plunged through the electric lit night
The night of crystal, the fog of smoke
What joyful noise that might come from pressed lips
Or the carefree rubbing of legs [if only]
A haunted music, an aching ghost

A bark sets out at the crossroads
Intersection of the visible & invisible made flesh
A clear case of phallocentric sadism
A' weepin' & a' pinin' fer love, as the old song goes
As the old song went: tonight, the bottle let me down

Baptism of red piss in a white urinal
Turgid itch & the perfume of death
Even the woods floating in air make blue shadows
Where exists a strong tone of "ironic disillusionment"
[The words begin to turn on themselves, knives raised]

Tonight, the bottle let me down
What lost its teeth bleeding under neon lights
Ideologically vague, temperamentally libertarian, joyfully nihilistic
Remorse is a pathology of syntax
Metaphors of pastures; anabasis & return
All the tenderest parts of the body are dismantled
We smoke our friends to the very filter
Tonight, the bottle let me down
Tonight, the bottle let me down

Personal Jesus
Depeche Mode

beneath & between the narcissus roots
figured a way to be a religious animal
connected by dreams, lust, & wires to Ultravox
    — half Essex, half Martian —
a hobo gospel song glazed w/ industrial heat
so mystical & soulful
going down on my knees
begging you to adore me
[your own personal Jesus]

now I'm not looking for absolution
forgiveness for the things I do
I give in to sin as I practise what I preach
where heaven waits / those golden gates
angels w/ silver wings / shouldn't know suffering
hush, can you feel the trees so far away?
words are so [very] (*un*)necessary
I've been a martyr for love
reach out & touch me
[your own personal Jesus]

(You're a) Strange Animal
Gowan

I've seen the low sun fearful with mystic signs
Enigmatic images that serve to penetrate the lizard brain
A vision of Christ hunkered down, napping, awaiting destiny
I mean, what is music w/o the ghost of another in it?
Ascending & descending the black mountain's side
Not seeking penetration but interpenetration
Under hands that grope for the shape of an animal unknown
A "modern primitive" shaman painted & dressed in white
With geometric markings in black on the face
Lidless eater of raw meat plucking music from a meatless rib
A mouth like the backside of a chicken

[I remember once I myself was a small animal, a faint
Quickness in the thicket; a sleek entity of mortarless enjambments
Running bare-assed & Fyodor Dostoevsky–like through the tall grass]

Must learn to think in stitches, in loose threads of hilarity
Along with the faint aromas of sex & phenobarbital
Must learn to speak a language with the fat & gristle
Of other languages showing through
Ghost autos rusted belly up in blue ditches
That you do me slowly almost not at all that you are my mouth
Pushes the track from moody to tempestuous: the peripheral flesh
Compact, homogenous, & a splendid chemical red
Finally, its nature is not grammatological but pneumatological
A case of having to screw a little thing I have to screw
O Ominous Spiritus!
Man, you're a strange animal

Love Is the Law
The Suburbs

"What we can't think for ourselves, we can always quote."
— LUDWIG WITTGENSTEIN

It's [another] beautiful day in the neighbourhood
A boy on a skateboard speeds downhill in the drive
A little girl in a blue dress holds a white cat with brown markings
Half-naked lotioned bodies piled on slatted plastic Adirondacks
    begin to melt or else move larval-like beneath the swelter of
        summer heat toward portable beer coolers & BBQs
"Love[ly] & true they are to the ways of flesh, flash, & [l]awe," I sd
The ear at work [here] is remarkably attuned
    to both sophistical & ordinary speech
      a more edgy [edgier] heteroglossia
Where Wittgenstein is especially admired for his plumbing
& carpentry skills
Connected by apophenia

(the genetic tendency to find patterns in coincidence that allows the discovery of conspiracy in any significant event; a feeling of abnormal meaningfulness. Conspiracy theories once limited to fringe audiences have become more commonplace in mass media — the concept of a pure accident is not permitted in a news item as it is no longer considered to be either news or newsworthy — & contribute as an emerging cultural phenomenon in the United States & Canada, i.e., **COVID-19 Is a Head Game** & the result of an "infodemic." **The National Organization of the Anvil** is the name of a former secret society of Mexican regional origin but alleged now to be an international political force & whose purpose is to defend the Catholic religion & fight the forces of Satan, whether through violence or murder. **Lizard People Have Taken Over** is a very old trope with disturbing

79

links to anti-immigrant & antisemitic hostilities dating to the 19th century. **The Protocols of the Learned Elders of Zion** is a hoaxed antisemitic book that purported to reveal a Jewish conspiracy to achieve world domination. **Operation Snow White** ((code name for an alleged criminal conspiracy by the Church of Scientology during the 1970s to purge unfavourable records while installing fake records that claim the benefits of worship about Scientology & its founder, L. Ron Hubbard. This project included a series of infiltrations, wiretappings, & thefts from the IRS, the FBI, & even CIA operations, using up to 5,000 covert agents)). **The casus belli** ((from the Latin meaning "occasion for war" is an act or an event that either provokes or is used to justify a war)). **Tupac Isn't Really Dead. The Moon Landing Was Filmed in Hollywood. The Satanic Panic. White Replacement Theory. COVID & 5G. Chemtrails Are Government Poison. The Alaskan Mind-Control Lab. Snapple & the Ku Klux Klan. Area 51. Hollow Earth Theory. Birds Aren't Real. The Greenbelt Is a Scam. Language Is a Virus from Outer Space.** &ETC. Conspiracy is a particular narrative form of scapegoating that frames demonized enemies as part of a vast insidious plot against the common good, wherein one blames the "outside forces" rather than oneself. Other popular knowledge might include alien abduction stories, magazine gossip, certain new age philosophies, religious beliefs, astrology. Studies have found that conspiracy theorists frequently believe in multiple conspiracies even when one conspiracy contradicts the other. Conspiracy theories are often labelled as the "exhaust fumes of democracy.")

I mean, whose traffic jam is whose?
If you open any window an alarm sounds & sirens follow
Oh elusive sleep where hast thou gone thou fuck
I ordered pompoms online & received [instead, postage paid]

a kind of rapid-firing machine gun. Didn't complain,
            didn't return, didn't . . . simply added it to the growing
                    arsenal stowed in the attic, in the basement, as a
                    sort of
                        "just in case" doomsday scenario

                    (Long ago this story had many birds & I
                    ambled passing branch to branch, going into
                    somersault, revised & held thereafter, ah,
                    looking down, slow crash at twilight angles,
                    slow fall to grasses in the winter snow)

It's [another] beautiful day in the neighbourhood
A boy on a skateboard speeds downhill in the drive
A little girl in a blue dress holds a white cat with brown markings
Half-naked lotioned bodies piled on slatted plastic Adirondacks
        begin to melt or else move larval-like beneath the swelter of
                summer heat toward beer coolers & BBQs
"Love[ly] & true they are to the ways of flesh, flash, & [l]awe," I sd

Ain't No Sunshine
Bill Withers

separation begins with placement
a series of sharply observed miniatures
rendered aslant
a portrait void of appearance
yet replete with animal gait
the underpart is, though stemmed, uncertain
tigerish things are occurring
love is form & cannot be without
jammed stuck — the entire block & tackle
of the inner workings —
let it bleed, let it weep
black describes the feeling
what's rolled in since she's been gone:
  mountain fog, sea fog, ice fog of the arctic
warp & woof ravel in the afterglow

  oh, I don't know what I don't know, no
  oh, I don't know what I don't know, no
  oh, I don't know what I don't know, no
  oh, I don't know what I don't know, no
  oh, I don't know what I don't know, no
  oh, I don't know what I don't know, no

can one miss what one never had?
undoubtedly, constantly
you are the sunflower crazed with light
a one composed of nudity & laughter
a dizzying vortex of beating wings
& flying drapery
the fume of a fine whiskey, eyes alive
as a pair of lit cigarettes
who never claimed to be a green thing
in a quiet home

where nothing happens but the wallpaper
let it bleed, let it weep
black describes the feeling
what's rolled in since she's been gone:
       mountain fog, sea fog, ice fog of the arctic
warp & woof ravel in the afterglow
hey, let's cut to the chase
stock image of young tanned legs
disappearing into clear blue lake water
another [lousy, sure]
"somebody done somebody wrong song"
let it bleed, let it weep
black describes the feeling
oh, I don't know what I don't know, no
oh, I don't know what I don't know, no

Life in a Northern Town
The Dream Academy

rainy day w/ yellow warblers & wild canaries
things take their immutable course w/ calculated movements
completely predictable, no fireworks
life is a series of destructions
ah, hey, yeah, yeah, ya-yeah, ah, hey, yeah
with its fading pink bricks & worn houses
the scene contains something dry & evil about it
a delicate touch of horror
rooms of uninhabited furniture
four small sausages shining in gelatin spread over a bed of parsley
a teacup vagina encircled in fur
undertones of corruption & decadence
      in the middle-class suburban lifestyle
          that exemplifies the American dream
ah, hey, yeah, yeah, ya-yeah, ah, hey, yeah
an army of youth bearing the standard of truth
chanting "Safe in the Arms of Jesus"
[slow-rolling bass line & piano counterpoint the chiming riffs
& falsetto chorus w/ plenty of gravitas]
migration of geese overhead
a river (or what might just as well be a river)
a jagged line of misty peaks
a dirty undershirted guy smokes roll-yer-owns on the porch
a six-pack of Bud Light at his feet
a blue plastic transistor radio wrapped in grey duct tape
tuned in to Ruggero Leoncavallo's *Pagliacci* —
      "No! Pagliaccio non son! Se il viso è pallido, è di vergogna"
      "No! I'm not a clown! If my face is pale, it's from shame"
entrapment is this country's sole activity, I whisper, & only laughter
can blow it all to rags
but hey, if shit had value, the poor wouldn't have assholes, so
[don't forget yr lunch, be good, love mother]
ah, hey, yeah, yeah, ya-yeah, ah, hey, yeah

we buried the north together
rubble of slash, tailing piles, the bones of factories
who threw his horse into a gallop & crossed the bridge screaming
white legs disappearing into blue water
ah, hey, yeah, yeah, ya-yeah
ah, hey, yeah

Fade to Grey
Visage

Fondu au gris
Fondu au gris

Existing in a strange liminal space
The protagonist is awake, this much the protagonist knows
Loomed over like a serial killer or a question mark
A one who seeks isolation, acute social withdrawal
A weightlifter & poet with a trim midsection & broad lats

Qui est ce grand corbeau noir?
Près des roses du martyre le lis de la virginité
La terre est bleue comme une orange
La nuit, tous les chats sont gris

Who is this big black crow?
Near the roses of martyrdom the lily of virginity
The earth is as blue as an orange
At night, all cats are grey

Fondu au gris (aaah . . .)
[We] fade to grey (fade to grey)

Linked to the New Romantic fashion movement
Stepped out from the back pages of a glossy magazine
Disclosure seductively defers itself
Middle-aged, unnerved, subject to frequent bouts of dyspepsia
A zipper unzips & out falls a handful of dust & rubble
A life turned grey by imperceptible degrees

Fondu au gris (aaah . . .)
[We] fade to grey (fade to grey)

[I Never Promised You a] Rose Garden
Lynn Anderson

What'd you expect?
I'm at no centre big & slack as I am
Driven under the influence, say
The paratactic quality of the modernist lyric
Slightly filthy with erotic mystery
The music poignant, downhearted, emotional, & bruised
A pandemonium of paradoxical symmetries
Watch as I metamorphose effortlessly
From human to machine
In my evil nature, in the whole blue funk
A willing victim of commodity fetishism
[Do I have anything on at night? Yeah, the radio]

But, hey, hard-on
You've got your hand on my tit, that's it
Get the lumber off your shoulder
Dial it up, phone it in
At each step complication gains rewards
Who knows, maybe later I'll say maybe later
Beyond that, you know I'm lying
'Cause my lips are moving, yeah?
What can I tell you, my lover, my killer
Every particle has an antiparticle with which to annihilate
Gotta learn: take the pleasure with the pain
[From now on all of my friends are gonna be strangers]

Talk is cheap, still waters run deep, fine
Heartbreak aside we straddle that brittle edge
Bodies hung with trim paragraphs of uninflected speech
Self-modifiable software, inviolate hardware
On the other side an orga[ni]sm adrift in the void
A strangely unadapted being who loves things that
End badly & are monstrous

Am I become [then] "latent" or "figurative" in the mix?
Love grows fur in the oddest places
An impasto that evokes crusted clotted excretions
A bloodline for cutting horses
Still, unusual frankness shouldn't constitute obscenity
Should it
Look & you'll discover corridors of meaning
If I promise to kiss you will you [just] go away
[If I kiss you [will you [just] go away]]

I Ran [So Far Away]
A Flock of Seagulls

I wander the streets to be alone
never thinking, never thinking
modern love is [so] automatic
with its never-ending theme of
>   *. . . the prepubescent female combined with a sensual*
>   *Lolita-like provocativeness that repels as it attracts . . .*

practitioner of the zigzagging glance
your eyes, your eyes are nuclear & dangerous
& I ran, I ran so far away [I couldn't get away]
are you a wind instrument, are you breath?
syntax erupts & flows lubriciously
around its conventionally obstruent limitations
not exactly a moment of Wittgensteinian revelation, still
mechanical lyrics about a mechanical end to the world
application of the cinematic frame to language
a twilight zone of tawdry horror & sci-fi
— careful, you're sucking up my oxygen —
& I ran, I ran so far away [I couldn't get away]
looking back over your atomic shoulder
you play a beam of alabaster across your face
give me your hand, try to find some surface of yourself
that doesn't impose too much upon
too late, too late
on a shaft of light we enter the eternal machinery of the sky
borne away in a shower of radioactive dust
& I ran, I ran so far away [I couldn't get away]

I Ran [So Far Away]: A Transcription
A Flock of Seagulls

"Does anybody else consider this song a classic
of the '80s or is it just me?"

— JONATHAN BRAVO

. . . "fronted by a singer-synth player with a haircut stranger than anything you'd be likely to encounter in a month of poodle shows, A Flock of Seagulls strikes gold on the first try" [Parke Puterbaugh] . . . the new wave synth-pop song moves at a quick tempo of 145 beats per minute — makes me think of the double-time device in mid-'50s bop, Art Blakey, et al., Brubeck with a real hold on narrowing & thickening the line — with a chorus procession of A-G-A-G in the verses & F-G-A in the choruses; the song is written in the key of A minor . . . "great fun & a wonderful [bit] of new wave ear candy" [Tom Demalon] . . . during the song's introduction & musical interludes, short guitar riffs are played which make use of echo . . . "so transparently, guilelessly expedient that it actually provides the hook-chocked fun most current pop bands only advertise" [Robert Christgau] . . . "pioneering sounds, compelling hooks, & undeniably addictive gimmicks" [various] . . . you need a chorus, some distortion, & a delay with the delay time set to 350 milliseconds & a lot of echo (at least for the first part) . . . keyboard intro: A & G . . . scratch the 4th & 5th strings to make the Seagull Effect (use the delay! — play the chord & mute it almost immediately) . . . (this next chord let ring) . . . opening verse: "I walked along the avenue" (try to mute this one) . . . now for the chorus (just follow the voice): "& I *r a a an*, I ran so far away" . . . (it's the same for "I just ran, I ran all night & day") . . . listen to the song to know what parts to repeat — disclosure seductively defers itself; slippage is a primary modus operandi, the word "eyes" slides into "hypnotize" & "areola" gives way to "aurora borealis" — (after the chorus comes the intro again, with the space-age delay & then the verse again) . . . here comes the solo, play this very fast, muting at first & gradually letting go of the string so that at the end it's ringing . . . when the voice comes again, play the intro chords & also scratch the strings for the Seagull

Effect again, then play the normal verse figure & the chorus, & after the chorus comes the finale: play this a couple of times, then this, & then this, with the last chord played like the intro . . . that's it, enjoy . . .

Pissed Off 2AM
Alejandro Escovedo

the rain teaches us things
it's night & the rain is falling
ah, nights are for dreaming
don't you think?
in manganese & viridian oyster
w/ emerald
[my god, but it reeks of semen
& vaginal juices in here]
my poor silent friend, hey —
don't look so gloomy, babe
it's only two a.m.
I've been blind until now
      let's put the boots to
      these walls we've built
      let's cut the cunning lingo
      let's proceed by means
      of a sensitive empiricism
      where disclosure seductively
      defers itself
      to imagine a language
      is to imagine a form of life
      "gray" slides into "gravity"
      "gladioli" gives way to
      a bouquet of "gladiators"
my Spanish has Latin & Italian
has Taíno, Ciboney, Chichimeca
is a product of lingual whores
& linguistic infleshing
if it is consistent it is incomplete
if complete then inconsistent
let's suppose for a moment
a new tribe bound by gossip
& rumour of divine decadence

the condor ablaze
black-lighting the Andes
back-alley racket stench
of gut-stringed gauchos
where holiness is never found
[my god, but it reeks of semen
& vaginal juices in here]
extrapolation leads us to open doors
that were once bricked up
my poor silent friend, hey —
don't look so gloomy, babe
it's only two a.m.
I've been blind until now
        let's put the boots to
        these walls we've built
        let's cut the cunning lingo
[but ask me questions, please
I don't mean to bore you]
the radio is filled w/ electricity
as I am filled with the spirit agave
time [perhaps] to lace the shoes
& drive the dogs back
into the shadows
my poor silent friend, hey —
don't look so gloomy, babe
it's only two a.m.
[my god, but it reeks of semen
& vaginal juices in here]
no hay problema
it means nothing to me now
it means nothing to me now
it's only two a.m.

California Dreamin'
The Mamas & the Papas

up to my neck in catastrophes & petty sadnesses
these smells, these trees, this sidewalk
my body wrapped in a tattered blue raincoat
the scene is yellow & cold & on the soundtrack
small birds beat their wings
an icy wind eats between the concrete buildings
I stumble into a public toilet, fall to my knees
& begin to vomit
everything is a projection of a forlorn kind:
        "el desaliento y la angustia consumen mi corazón"
        "dejection & angst consume my heart"
everything is the product of a system of signification
L.A. a nocturnal emission
"summer of love" the memory of a memory
— note the distinction between the signifier & the signified —
the use of temporal & non-systematic configurations
of modular elements
"the logical picture of the facts is the thought," sd Wittgenstein
strange & frozen bathrooms where the plumbing works
according to an unexpected mechanism
so to dream & to age a winter the snow blows any which way
I take fright & am amazed to see myself here rather than there
I'm not the same anymore
        the present divides equally in two:
        that which is at hand & that which lies outside
my girl is the rain & snow pelting
    who comes bleached-blonde through the black air
        the stranger observed, breasts freshly pink from a steamy bath
phonemic density coupled with semantic openness
a hole in the roof where the rain comes in

Roxy Roller

Sweeney Todd

Blest with a mindset embedded
in the zeitgeist of the mid-'70s
made the transition from associationist
psychology to Darwinian functionalism
where the gaze is everything
is controlled & prescribed
moderately cryptic & mercilessly succinct
leaned contrapposto against the wall
a Dante-*esque* scene, just bodies from hell
all intertwined & asleep, covered in mud
a panoply of febrile lines & shadowy greys
[oh, saints are holy only when you roll 'em]
oh, oh, oh, Roxy Roller
oh, oh, oh, Roxy Roller

She is abuzz, is ashimmer, she vacillates
[that is] her being is in motion in love & out
all the cursing & crying & shouting
all the movement, the rash movement & so on
whose abstract nature provokes
our representational inclinations
a temple of greased palms & busted kneecaps
so to cleanse that stinking that has that odour
so to cleanse that the feathers are empty
so to drop the underwear as the Vox Humana swells
an ominous noir-like score with blaring horns
[oh, saints are holy only when you roll 'em]
oh, oh, oh, Roxy Roller
oh, oh, oh, Roxy Roller

Perdido
Ella Fitzgerald

lost, sloppy, or indecent
busted down on Perdido Street
where holiness is never found
enamoured of the salty-lipped toritos
no suspension of disbelief, but [instead]
a position of considered engagement
a rightful anticipation & sexuality
mixed with trepidation & fear
throw us a kiss then, cowboy mouth
& say adios
dreams are wish fulfillment, are fleeting
love is a [tragic] mix of sentimentality & sex
I just happened to board a train headed
in the wrong direction is all
a path of loose inclines & missing luggage
the odour of horse piss mixed with that of impatiens
sexual apparatus sewn shut & wrapped in cellophane
damned don't cry, yeah?
still, deep unexpected currents of dewy-eyed pathos
flow through the vista
dusk insinuates itself slowly
moths hover with the obstinance of ghosts
every limitation is a door to another form of misunderstanding
lost, sloppy, or indecent
an[other] hapless victim of the zipless fuck
throw us a kiss then, cowboy mouth
& say adios
goodnight Perdido, adios, so long

Hot for Teacher
Van Halen

under threat of epistemological slippage :: cursed with a sort of steampunk autonomic nervous system complete with flapping louvres & retinal scans :: who seek artistic agency through anarchic dismissal & revolt against consumer culture & fine art rarification :: enraptured agents of libidinous freedom within an atmosphere of pop glamour & celebrity fetishism :: sporting shaggy hair, bad skin, & T-shirts that read "I flunked the Voight-Kampff test" :: who struggle with a sense of educational failure & deficit, obsessed with equity because they were regarded as physically unattractive runts during preadolescence (a desperately scuzzy, dilapidated, tragicomic vision, for sure), hence, were never immune to the lure of flesh & glitz & awe :: it begins with an athletic thirty-second drum solo followed by another thirty seconds of instrumental intro :: extended guitar (1958 Gibson Flying V) that transitions into a thick principal riff :: multi-watt voltage surges through this speeding hard rock anthem :: rhapsodic swerve toward disintegration :: vocals that are spoken more than sung, two interlocked solos :: neither an emotion, nor yet a lip-synch of longing :: twilights of sexuality & inattention :: lyrics that are technically demeaning but somehow come across as non-toxic & guileless :: a narration of spatial perception :: a universe of clichés so familiar that they seem at once comforting & strange :: *[careful, I understand that I'm in hostile territory here, blame my complex Presbyterian anti-authoritarian lesbian feminist radical centrism upbringing alongside an emergent theme of unsettling otherness, but, hey, I must seek significance where I can find it, yes? :: note to self, maybe time to scrape the dogma from the bottom of my sole & entertain the "complex engagement approach" toward so-called outlaw behaviour]* :: a universe tethered to the corporeal form, a fulcrum between scales of the heavenly body & temptations of its earthly delights :: [nota bene, "at the basis of all Christian rhetoric is an unnatural fear of sex"] :: transition from the commerce of bodies to the commerce of contracted bodies :: the fluidity between pictorialism & textuality :: a discursive, visceral wondering, its burlesque-laden female figure(s) executed in swirling greens, blues, & pinks, tearing off [t]he[i]r costume to reveal a hot bikinied body to a classroom of unruly, hormonally charged, cheering young students :: an[other] obvious case of cultural cannibalism :: so pleasurably flesh, it says, & dwells among us, flesh offered to flesh :: the flexibility of the composition as a container of meaning :: a shift to appropriating positions & functions :: a slight detachment, a slight separation which forms a complete coloured picture :: darker, more complex songs in minor keys :: the song ending comes from a drum-heavy studio demo by way of the band's club days titled "Voodoo Queen" :: got it bad, got it bad, got it bad . . .

Fun facts:
An initial controversy arose when the video showed all the band members (dressed in red outfits and dancing beneath a disco ball) performing a quick crotch grab during the "*so* bad" part of the chorus; at first, the 1980s NBC late-night show *Friday Night Videos* added black-box censor bars to the crotch grabs but eventually relented and removed the black box from their video.

If you take the numbers written on the chalkboard behind teacher and exchange them for their positions in the alphabet, they read "Holy Shit."

At the video's end, we are told that the young boy band members grew up to become a gynecologist, a sumo wrestler, a patient in a mental institution, and a popular game show host. The class nerd grew up to be a successful pimp.

Meanwhile, there were *two* "teachers" in the video. Lillian Müller was a "Page Three Girl" five times, as well as a *Playboy* Playmate of the Year in 1976, followed by nine further *Playboy* cover features. Additionally, she was voted Sexiest Vegetarian Over 50. She is currently an inspirational speaker and personal health consultant. Donna Rupert was a former Miss Canada pageant runner-up, who went on to star in numerous TV commercials. She also established her own clothing line for children. She is currently a successful landscape artist.

One More Song the Radio Won't Like
Kathleen Edwards

walking in the park, it's winter, looks like someone
got mugged in the snowy dawn, though . . .
gotta resist the obstinate retention of either the fixed idea
  or the three-dimensional diorama
    of events that [maybe] didn't happen
gotta make sure that thinking doesn't deteriorate into slop
gotta resist the primal impulse to thump & twang
I'm no *Indie "It" Girl*, I know
don't wanna be the four-chord singer-songwriter
don't wanna love someone no matter how fucked up they are
don't wanna *just* be something he can do with his hands
(interesting . . . the possibilities that are embedded in the scenery)
so what if he only pisses on the toilet seat?
a bastard who knows how to feign tenderness
another sad/lost case of bad debts & dirty laundry
bristling with graffiti & weather-beaten walls
the owner of thirty rifles, ten screwdrivers
  one blowtorch, an electric clock, an old
    faded photo of a long-dead hunting dog
a bear-shaped belt buckle that opens beer bottles
about as much mystique as finding a cockroach in your kitchen
but, hey, it's Christmas time (let's just survive)
a defence of dilapidated lace, screaming radios, & fake evergreens
c'mon, c'mon. ever fallen for a psychopath? someone
totally devoid of feelings, empathy, & remorse [yeah, me too]
there is no phenomenon that doesn't elicit its own interpretation
[though not all psychopaths are killers, they say (comforting to know, given)]
am I dancing here or dying? waving or drowning?
no one likes a girl who won't sober up, yeah?
who has an anti-psychiatric fascination with excrement, blood, & decay
all heroes start out in meadow dust & end up in the gutter, seems
but, hey, it's Christmas time (let's just survive)
where there are no solutions because there are no problems

why not pop a cold one, light up a Lucky, do a line
seal myself in a crack of air & swallow the key

Bonus
Tracks

[She's Come] Undun
The Guess Who

Guess who
    rendering the scene a pulse
        goes noumenal in the gloss.
At back, uranium lilts the lunar sea madly
Erotic, while foreground teases optic
Warp & woof
Cause
    for abstraction enough
Neverminding

> *she's come undone, didn't notice*
> *that the light had changed*

As here & there the beat & flicker tends bodies
Toward dissolve.
Ah, that old bordello moon altering love's bright
Promise, dances light to its light way
    & fashions figures that move abstractly
        naked not nude, recalling "we shoot nudes"
Emerges
    both reconciled & estranged amid the bud

> *now it's time to rearrange*

What might mistake a melon slice or drinks on a tray
Remains, otherwise, fairly constant:
    phosphor bronze catch of legs, ass, belly, breasts
    some snatch of mons veneris
    sweet aureole of nipple sounding out the mix
Portrays exotic in the clime.
Candy for any eye or ear
That serves to pound a steady line

Perverse, as:
          "The aberration of these faceless in a cloud.
          Petals spent on wet, black boughs"
Makes mutable

          light changed
              rearranged
                  she's come undone

Don't Explain
Billie Holiday

Whiskey blind, staggering home at five.
You wore thin bow ties, thick dark-rimmed glasses,
& sucked on peppermints to sweeten your breath.
Some men take their liquor slow and count : *who?*
— a nasty mix of cold dice & hot jazz —
(skip the lipstick, don't explain)

Oh, I know who you are you, you used to be
someone, someone who had a friend who had a
sister who . . . but, my God, you didn't need to
undress everyone, did you?
Sweet *daddy-o*, chief inspector of holes
(skip the lipstick, don't explain)

That two bits of twilight that you spoke
(fine, fine, okay, you can't help yourself)
just — for decorum's sake, anyway —
keep your hands where I can see 'em, yeah?
In the air & off the merchandise
(skip the lipstick, don't explain)

No argument I was not involved personally (only)
I am a twenty-five-year-old woman & thus
do engage in regular sexual intercourse.
Liquid constantly oozes & soaks my panties.
Christ, is that thing alive? I hear a hungry roar
(skip the lipstick, don't explain)

In other words, what I mean is
— but there are no other words —
you know I must leave you & I can't.
Let's assume I've gained something in the process.
If not, *boo-hoo*, *boo-hoo*, poor me
(skip the lipstick, don't explain)

Words speak less than a grimace & a twitch.
Go, bring me the sunflower crazed with light
(it's the sort of thing a princess always says).
Whatever : love grows fur in the strangest places.
& a girl? A girl soon grows tired of roses.
Gimme a pig foot & a bottle of beer.
Gimme a reason to sing the blues
(skip the lipstick, don't explain)

We Had It Made

Natalee (Nat) Slagor

What up, babe? What up with you?
We had it once, now we're through.
It wasn't me, so that leaves who?
You vanished darlin', without a clue.
It's tits up & bugger you.
Tra-lah, la-lah, tra-lah, la-lah, la-lah.
Tra-lah, la-lah, tra-lah, la-lah, la-lah.
What we had fit like a glove.
What we had was push to shove.
What we had was . . . whatever . . .
Call it fate, call it over, okay, I called it love.
We had it made [not really].
We had it made [not really].
O, O, O, O, O, O.
O, O, O, O, O, O.
You are gone, but you won't fade.
Like a needle in a vein.
Like a tattoo on my brain.
What we had fit like a glove.
What we had was push to shove.
What we had was . . . whatever . . .
Call it fate, call it over, okay, I called it love.
Tra-lah, la-lah, tra-lah, la-lah, la-lah.
Tra-lah, la-lah, tra-lah, la-lah, la-lah.
It's tits up & bugger you.
O, O, O, O, O, O.
O, O, O, O, O, O.
We had it made [not really].
We had it made [not really].
We had it made [not really].
(fade)

Song for a Rose
Traditional

(opens with Spanish guitar solo, played andante)

She spoke about a tiger that turned out to be a rose
& about the fur that exists beneath our clothes
She purred a deep contentment until our bodies froze

What does it really matter when it all turns out the same
You peel away the layers & are left with what remains

Our listening was intense as we huddled in the blind
Triggers cocked in vain & the layers we would find
Astonished by resemblances & the layers we would find

What does it really matter when it all turns out the same
You peel away the layers & are left with what remains

We made love & marvelled upon the jungled sheets
The fragrant scent of tigers receded in the heat
Claws of bloody roses painted on our cheeks

*(instrumental break with guitar, horns, & strings, played more
uplifting & allegro)*

You peel away the layers & are left with what remains
No matter how you feel it, it all turns out the same
What does it really matter if it all turns out the same

(repeats . . .)

Entertainment. Writing. Culture. ────────────

ECW is a proudly independent, Canadian-owned book publisher. We know great writing can improve people's lives, and we're passionate about sharing original, exciting, and insightful writing across genres.

──────────────────────── **Thanks for reading along!**

We want our books not just to sustain our imaginations, but to help construct a healthier, more just world, and so we've become a certified B Corporation, meaning we meet a high standard of social and environmental responsibility — and we're going to keep aiming higher. We believe books can drive change, but the way we make them can too.

Certified

Corporation

Being a B Corp means that the act of publishing this book should be a force for good — for the planet, for our communities, and for the people that worked to make this book. For example, everyone who worked on this book was paid at least a living wage. You can learn more at the Ontario Living Wage Network.

This book is also available as a Global Certified Accessible™ (GCA) ebook. ECW Press's ebooks are screen reader friendly and are built to meet the needs of those who are unable to read standard print due to blindness, low vision, dyslexia, or a physical disability.

The interior of this book is printed on Sustana Opaque™, which is made from 30% recycled fibres and processed chlorine-free.

FSC

ECW's office is situated on land that was the traditional territory of many nations, including the Wendat, the Anishnaabeg, Haudenosaunee, Chippewa, Métis, and current treaty holders the Mississaugas of the Credit. In the 1880s, the land was developed as part of a growing community around St. Matthew's Anglican and other churches. Starting in the 1950s, our neighbourhood was transformed by immigrants fleeing the Vietnam War and Chinese Canadians dispossessed by the building of Nathan Phillips Square and the subsequent rise in real estate value in other Chinatowns. We are grateful to those who cared for the land before us and are proud to be working amidst this mix of cultures.

ecwpress.com